XVII   Monographs on Archaeology and the Fine Arts

Sponsored by   The Archaeological Institute of America and

The College Art Association of America

Monographs Editor, *Bates Lowry*

The publication of this Monograph

has been aided by a grant from

The Samuel H. Kress Foundation

Bernini and the Crossing of Saint Peter's

Irving Lavin

New York University

1968

Published for The College Art Association of America

by New York University Press   New York, N.Y.

Copyeditor: *Miriam R. Koren*

Designer: *Malcolm Grear*

Typesetter: *Connecticut Printers, Inc.*

Printer: *Eastern Press, Inc.*

Library of Congress Catalog Card Number: 68-22570

To My Father

Preface

I am conscious of a special debt to the work of Hans Kauffmann, who in a series of studies of Bernini's sources has virtually opened a new approach to his art. Several of the conclusions reached here have their origin in observations made by Kauffmann (in "Berninis Tabernakel," *MünchJb*, 6, 1955, 366–374, and "Berninis Hl. Longinus," in *Miscellaneae Bibliothecae Hertzianae,* Munich, 1961, 222–242), and I am glad to add this general acknowledgment to the individual ones given in the footnotes. I have also profited greatly, for the period preceding Urban VIII, from the survey of the decoration of Saint Peter's by Herbert Siebenhüner ("Umrisse zur Geschichte der Ausstattung von St. Peter," in *Festschrift für Hans Sedlmayr,* Munich, 1962, 229–320). Howard Hibbard read the manuscript and made a number of valuable suggestions, as did Bates Lowry, editor of *The Art Bulletin.* No attempt will be made here to deal with every aspect of the decoration of the crossing; for Borromini's contribution in particular the reader is referred to the forthcoming publication of his drawings by Heinrich Thelen.

I should like to express my gratitude to Ingegnere Francesco Vacchini of the Reverenda Fabbrica di San Pietro, and to his assistant Sig. Mario Pirolli for many favors granted in connection with this study. The research was facilitated by the ready cooperation and assistance of D. Cipriano Maria dott. Cipriani, archivist of the Fabbrica. A large part of the work was carried out while I was the holder of a Fellowship of the American Council of Learned Societies, for which I am most grateful. The manuscript was completed in June, 1966, except for some minor bibliographical additions.

A number of items that appeared or came to my attention after the manuscript was set in type are noted in the Addenda. A study by H. Thelen dealing with the history of the high altar and baldachin (*Zur Entstehungsgeschichte der Hochaltar-Architektur von St. Peter in Rom,* Berlin, 1967) became available too late to be taken into account.

ROME, JUNE, 1968

Contents

Text Figure

Disposition of the Relics in the Crossing (detail from plan of Saint Peter's from C. Fontana, *Templum vaticanum et ipsius origo,* Rome, 1694, pl. following p. 380):

Introduction

In the present essay "the crossing of Saint Peter's" refers to the grandiose plan by which, during the reign of Pope Urban VIII (1623–1644) under Bernini's direction, a visually and conceptually unified focus was created at the tomb of the Prince of the Apostles (Fig. 1).[1] The scheme consisted essentially of grouping four of the major relics of early Christianity, previously dispersed, about the altar above the tomb.[2] My chief purpose here is to define the way in which the arrangement was given meaning and expressive form in the baldachin above the altar and in the decorations of the four piers supporting the dome of the basilica. It will be necessary to consider also the earlier contributions, which conditioned the final solution, and the changes introduced in the course of execution, as a result of which much of the original unity was lost. Chapters I–IV trace the broad outlines of the history of the crossing through the period in question, with emphasis on the sources and meaning of the baldachin. Chapter V analyzes the role of the colossal statues in the lower niches of the piers. The Conclusion (Chapter VI) is a schematic and tentative effort to understand the significance of the crossing in Bernini's development. The Appendices offer an annotated list of projects submitted before and in competition with Bernini.

1. A tradition universally accepted since the Middle Ages held that the bodies of both St. Peter and St. Paul had been divided; half of each had been deposited at Saint Peter's, the other two halves at Saint Paul's Outside the Walls (cf. E. Kirschbaum, *The Tombs of St. Peter & St. Paul*, London, 1959, 209ff.). For effects of the legend on planning for the crossing see nn.48, 111, 171 below.

2. For the holy days and special occasions on which the Passion relics are shown, see Moroni, *Dizionario*, CIII, 101f. In 1964 the head of St. Andrew was returned to Patras in Greece, whence it had come to Rome under Pius II in 1462 (*L'Osservatore Romano*, anno 104, No. 218, Sept. 20, 1964, 4, and subsequent issues; see now R. O. Rubenstein, "Pius II's Piazza S. Pietro and St. Andrew's Head," in *Essays in the History of Architecture Presented to Rudolf Wittkower*, London, 1967, 22ff.). See also end of n.125 below.

I. The Crossing Before Bernini

THE PIERS

The first steps toward the new disposition of the relics may be said to have been taken under Pope Paul V (1605–1621). In 1606, with the destruction of the nave of the old basilica, Paul transferred the three chief relics that had long been in Saint Peter's to the two piers flanking the apse of the new building:[3] the Holy Face (Volto Santo) and the Lance of St. Longinus were moved to the southwest pier, the head of St. Andrew to the northwest (Text Fig. A; see p. 24).[4] The relics were kept in the upper niches, which were separated from the larger niches below by balconies with balustrades (Figs. 2–4).[5] The arrangement thus retained, without altars below, that of the two-story free-standing tabernacles which had been among the most prominent monuments in Old Saint Peter's (Figs. 7–9).[6] Until Bernini's time, the lower niche of the southeast pier contained the tomb of Paul III (1534–1549), while before the northeast pier stood the famous Colonna Santa, the spiral column against which Christ was believed to have leaned in the Temple at Jerusalem (Text Fig. A).[7]

The permanent decoration of the niches seems to have been undistinguished. In engravings showing the crossing during the great quintuple canonization of 1622, however, the upper reliquary niches contain hangings (Figs. 5, 6).[8] These are doubtless the same as two paintings—one with Sts. Peter and Paul holding aloft the Volto Santo, the other showing St. Andrew with his cross—which had been given to the basilica a decade before.[9] The use of the paintings in the niches is of consid-

3. Evidently there was an earlier plan, not carried out, to reorganize the display of the relics in the new church: "Si tratta di fare nel fenestrone principale della gran tribuna del nuovo San Pietro un nuovo pulpito balaustrato con finiss.ᵉ pietre, reliquie del volto santo et lancia di nostro Sig.ʳᵉ . . ." (Avviso of Aug. 18, 1598) Cited by Orbaan, *Documenti*, 46f. n., whose transcription I have checked against the original. Siebenhüner, "Umrisse," 301, gratuitously interpolates a phrase into this passage, and interprets it as referring to the west window of the drum of the cupola.

4. The fundamental source for the transferral of the relics is Grimaldi, *Instrumenta autentica . . . 1619* (on Grimaldi, see Pastor, *History of the Popes*, XXVI, 382; henceforth cited as Pastor). Grimaldi also devoted a special treatise to the Volto Santo and the Lance, *Opusculum de sacrosancto Veronicae Sudario . . .*, 1618.
   All three relics were moved on Jan. 25, 1606, to the capitulary archive while the Veronica niche was being readied (*ibid.*, fols. 82ff.); they were moved thither on March 21 (*ibid.*, fols. 87ff.). This transferral is reported in an Avviso of March 25 (Orbaan, "Der Abbruch Alt-Sankt Peters 1605–1615," 48—henceforth references to Orbaan are to this work unless otherwise stated; and Orbaan, *Documenti*, 71). The head of St. Andrew was shifted to the northwest pier on Nov. 29, 1612 (Grimaldi, *Opusculum*, fols. 90v f.).

5. Cf. Appendix I Nos. 5f., 10, 14f. See also Ferrabosco, *Architettura*, pls. XIV, XXII.
   Payments during 1605–6 for work on the stairways within the piers, the balustrades, etc., are published by Pollak, "Ausgewählte Akten," 116, and Orbaan, 36ff.

6. Kauffmann was the first to note the relevance of the earlier tabernacles ("Berninis Tabernakel," 229ff.). According to Braun, *Der christliche Altar*, II, 259ff., tabernacles of this kind were characteristically Roman.
   The tabernacles occupied prominent positions in the old basilica. That of Saint Andrew, originally erected by Pius II (1458–64), stood just inside the façade in the southernmost aisle (cf. Alfarano, *De basilicae vaticanae*, 86f., No. 85 on the plan, pl. I). The Volto Santo tabernacle, dating from the twelfth century, stood in the corresponding position in the northernmost aisle (*ibid.*, 107f., No. 115 on the plan). The tabernacle of the Lance, built by Innocent VIII (1484–92) together with his famous tomb, was at the far end of the central nave at the south crossing pier (*ibid.*, 57ff., No. 38 on the plan). The Saint Andrew and Volto Santo tabernacles are shown *in situ* in another drawing in Grimaldi, *Instrumenta autentica* (reproduced by Orbaan, 13 fig. 5).
   It is interesting to note that in 1507, when the building of the new basilica began under Julius II, the Lance was transferred to the tabernacle of the Volto Santo (Alfarano, *De basil. vat.*, 58n., 108); they remained together when Paul V moved them to the crossing.

7. Cf. Panciroli, *Tesori nascosti*, 531f.

8. See pp. 8f. below; Appendix I Nos. 14, 15.

9. The donations are recorded by Grimaldi:
   1611. Illustrissimus R.ᵐᵘˢ Dñs Scipio Corbellutius S.R.E. Presbyter Cardinalis Sanctae Susannae tunc Vaticanae Basilicae Canonicus pia erga Sanctissimū Jesu Christi Sudarium religione motus, ante absidatā magnam fenestram, unde eadem sancta facies populo ostenditur yconam imaginibus, & Apostolorum Petri & Pauli coloribus expres-

erable interest, for it indicates that monumental representations of figures referring to the relics were part of the decoration of the piers, at least on special occasions, before Bernini began his transformation.

THE TOMB AND THE HIGH ALTAR

Before discussing the contributions made under Paul V at the tomb and high altar, we may review briefly the previous history of the shrine. Modern excavations combined with other evidence have made it possible to reconstruct with rare accuracy the monument as it had been installed by Constantine when he built Saint Peter's (Fig. 10).[10] It consisted of four twisted marble columns forming a screen across the apse; in front of the two central columns were placed two more twisted columns, creating a square enclosure around the tomb.[11] Two semicircular ribs intersecting diagonally rested on these four central columns. Around A.D. 600 drastic changes were introduced. The level of the apse floor was raised and a bench placed around it with a bishop's throne at the back (cf. Fig. 18). Over the tomb was placed a ciborium, whose design is unknown, except for the fact that it had four columns. The six original spiral columns were now arranged in a line in front of this presbytery, and in the eighth century another set of six was added in front of them, to form a second, outer screen (Fig. 11). The shrine remained essentially in this form until construction of the new basilica began in the early sixteenth century under Bramante. Bramante removed the outer row of columns, replacing them with the wall of a protective structure that incorporated the apse and enclosed the rest of the shrine (cf. Fig. 17). This structure stood until the time of Clement VIII (1592–1605). It was then removed to permit raising the floor level again and construction of the new *grotte*, or crypt. The high altar was also refurbished (dedicated 1594), and over it Clement erected a provisional ciborium with a cupola of wood.[12]

There reverberates throughout the subsequent history of the crossing a dilemma that was a direct consequence of having erected a centrally planned church over the tomb. Ancient tradition at Saint

---

sam dono dedit cū ūbella. (Opusculum, fols. 90r f.)

1612. Cum R.mus Dn's Angelus Damascenus Romanus utriusque signaturae sanctissimi Domini Nostri referendarius dictae Vaticanae Basilicae Canonicus ante fenestram magnam absidatam in parastata summi Tholi, ubi ex nobiliss.o marmoreo suggestu ad sinistram arae maximae caput sancti Andreae Apostoli populo ostenderetur, yconam cum imagine sancti Andreae Crucem amplectētis cū ūbella figuris & insignibus ornata pia largitione fecisset. (Ibid., fol. 90v)

10. B. M. Apollonj Ghetti, *et al.*, *Esplorazioni sotto la confessione di San Pietro in Vaticano*, Vatican City, 1951, 161ff. For a summary, see J. Toynbee and J. Ward Perkins, *The Shrine of St. Peter and the Vatican Excavations*, London-New York, 1956, 195ff.

11. On the spiral columns, see pp. 14ff. below.

12. See Orbaan, *Documenti*, 47n., 48n.; a first payment for the ciborium was made in June, 1594. Documents for the removal of the ciborium are cited in Orbaan, 44.

13. Quoted n.16 below.

14. See Appendix I Nos. 24, 25. The first objection to which Papirio Bartoli replies in his treatise describing his project is that it would take up too much room in the crossing (*Discorso*, int. 2, fol. 1ff.).

15. Owing to the subsequent retention of the choir begun by Nicolas V (Magnuson, *Roman Quattrocento Architecture*, 177f.), the tomb and high altar is not in the center of the crossing, but slightly to the west. Judging from the engraved plan by Dupérac, Michelangelo had planned to shift it in the opposite direction in order to achieve true centrality (cf. Siebenhüner, "Umrisse," 291).

16. The character and importance of this project was first defined by Siebenhüner, "Umrisse," 313f. The relevant passage in the Avviso is as follows:
   . . . sendosi intanto fatto levare quella cuppola di legno, che ci era in mezo della nuova chiesa sudetta sopra l'altare maggiore delli Santissimi Apostoli, quale altare anco si levarà secondo il nuovo modello, dovendosi trasportar più avanti verso il capo della chiesa, ove sarà il choro per poter et Sua Santita et il Sacro Colleggio intervenire alli divini officij, sentendosi, che dove hora è il detto altare, vi si farà una balaustrata intorno con scalini per potere scendere a basso et andar a celebrar messa all'altare et corpi de detti· Santi Apostoli, senza

Peter's, as elsewhere, required that the high altar be in close proximity to the apse, which served as a choir for the pope and the sacred college during solemn functions. No less important, however, was the traditional connection between the high altar and the tomb. Logically, only four solutions were possible, all of which were proposed or attempted at one time or another, but none of which could be wholly satisfactory. First, the high altar could be moved westward toward the apse, relinquishing its connection with the tomb. Second, the tomb might be moved along with the high altar, a course that ran the risk, as one source reports, of searching for the bodies of the apostles in vain, although it was known for sure that they were there.[13] Third, the tomb and high altar might be left *in situ* and a choir built around them, necessitating an inconvenient encumbrance of the crossing (Figs. 12, 13).[14] The fourth alternative was to leave the altar and tomb undisturbed, and relinquish the connection with the choir.

Of these possibilities the first and fourth are particularly important: the last because, having evidently been preferred by Michelangelo, it was finally resolved upon by Urban VIII and executed by Bernini;[15] the first because it was the one chosen at the beginning of Paul V's reign, and the projects for it, though never carried out in permanent form, profoundly influenced the design of Bernini's baldachin. The decision in favor of the first solution is reported in an Avviso of January 18, 1606, at the time the relics were being transferred to the new church.[16] According to this dispatch it had been determined to shift the high altar toward the main apse, where a choir would be installed. A proposal to move the tomb as well had been rejected, and instead stairs were planned to give access from the floor level down to the tomb so that mass could be said there; this was the beginning of the open "confessio" carried out later in Paul V's reign.[17] The second altar was actually built, and simultaneously a baldachin was erected over the original altar and a model of the proposed ciborium over the new one.[18]

The baldachin over the tomb altar, built of perishable materials, broke radically with tradition. At least since the late fifteenth century the ciboria over the high altar of Saint Peter's had conformed to a basic type, with four columns supporting a cupola (Figs. 15–18).[19] As we have noted, the tem-

moverli altrimenti, come alcuni altri volevano et è stato questo tenuto più salutifero consiglio, per non mettersi in pericolo di cercarli indarno, sebene si sa certo, che ci sono. (Orbaan, 44; Orbaan, *Documenti*, 68) Cf. also an Avviso of Oct. 4, 1606, in Armellini, *Le chiese di Roma,* 903.

17. The Florentine painter and architect Ludovico Cigoli submitted a project that involved moving the tomb (Figs. 25, 26; see p. 6f. below and Appendix I No. 18). A project by Martino Ferrabosco for a confessio with circular balustrade and stairways is recorded, though there is no certain evidence that he was in Rome by this date (see n.176 below).

18. Payments for the new altar are recorded as early as Dec., 1605: "per fare l'armatura de l'altare da fare nella tribuna grande verso Santa Marta . . . per ordine di messer Carlo Maderni" (Orbaan, 40). The altar over the tomb continued to function, though one project for a ciborium over the tomb seems to contemplate its removal (Fig. 14; Appendix I No. 2).

Payments for dismantling the ciborium of Clement VIII occur in Jan., 1606 (Orbaan, 44). Payments for building the new baldachin over the tomb altar begin in Feb. (Fraschetti, *Il Bernini*, 55f.; Pollak, "Ausgewählte Akten," 110; Orbaan, 45ff.). Payments for the model of the ciborium over the new altar at the choir begin in Sept. (*ibid.*, 54ff.).

The designer or designers of both these structures remain anonymous, though Carlo Maderno, as architect of the basilica, is the most likely candidate. Nevertheless, the phraseology of the document quoted at the beginning of this note is inconclusive, since Maderno may have ordered work to be done even though it was not of his invention.

19. For a general survey, see Braun, *Der christ. Altar,* II, 185ff.

The Saint Peter's ciborium is shown with a dome in: a medal of 1470 of Paul II celebrating his reconstruction of the tribune (Fig. 15; cf. G. Zippel, "Paolo II e l'arte," *L'Arte,* 14, 1911, 184f.; Magnuson, *Roman Quattrocento Architecture,* 169); a reconstruction by Grimaldi of the ciborium built by Sixtus IV (1471–84), of which important relief sculptures are preserved (Fig. 16); the *Donation of Constantine* fresco by the Raphael school in the Sala di Costantino in the Vatican (Fig. 17); a drawing by the Swiss pilgrim Sebastian Werro, who visited Rome in 1581 (Fig. 18); E. Wymann, "Die Aufzeichnungen des Stadtpfarrers Sebastian Werro von Freiburg i. Ue. über seinen Aufenthalt in Rom von 10–27. Mai 1581," *Römische Quartalschrift für christliche Altertumskunde und für Kirchengeschichte,* 33, 1925, 39ff.

porary ciborium of Clement VIII, which this new one replaced, also had a cupola.[20] In contrast to these predecessors, Paul V's baldachin, as recorded in many contemporary illustrations, consisted of a tasseled canopy supported on staves held by four standing angels (Figs. 2–4, 19–23);[21] it reproduced, in effect, a portable canopy such as was borne above bishops (hence the pope) on formal occasions, and above the Holy Sacrament and the relics of the Passion when they were carried in procession.[22] This was the basic theme that would be retained in the two subsequent baldachins built over the tomb, including Bernini's. The scale of the baldachin was impressive; its height has been calculated at roughly nine meters, only a meter short of Bernini's bronze columns.[23] Moreover, it was to be executed in bronze,[24] a significant innovation, since monumental altar coverings were usually of stone. The project thus foreshadows the material of Bernini's baldachin, as well as the underlying notion of translating a normally "ephemeral" type into permanent and monumental terms.

The purpose of this revolutionary design must have been largely symbolic. With the removal of the high altar the tomb itself became a kind of reliquary, for which such a canopy would be appropriate. At the same time, by alluding to the processional canopy traditionally associated with the bishop, the new design may have been intended to mark the special character of the site as the tomb of the first pope. Whatever its meaning, the baldachin offered a vivid and surely deliberate contrast to the proper ciborium that was at the same time erected over the new papal altar.

It should be noted, finally, that the depictions of the baldachin during the canonization of Carlo Borromeo in 1610 are of interest in showing the decorations it received for the occasion (Figs. 2, 3, 20).[25] Strands of lilies are wound spirally about the supports, and above the canopy proper is a medallion with an image of the saint, held in Giovanni Maggi's engraving by two kneeling angels (Fig. 2).[26]

In the Maggi engraving there also appears a partial view of the ciborium over the apse altar, jutting above the temporary arcade at the back of the enclosure (Fig. 24). It shows a polygonal structure whose dome rests on a high drum with volutes at the corners; the dome is surmounted by a lantern topped by a globe and cross. We know from other contemporary witnesses that the ciborium employed ten of the famous twisted columns that adorned the mediaeval sanctuary.[27] These pieces of information make it possible to link (though not identify) the model that was built with a group

---

20. See the Avviso of Jan. 18, 1606, quoted n.16 above, and another of Oct. 28, 1600, cited by Orbaan, *Documenti,* 48n. In an Avviso of June 29, 1594, it is described as "un ornamento di tavole depinto a similitudine di catafalco" (*ibid.,* 47n.).

21. Appendix I Nos. 4–12. Payments for the angels were made to the sculptors Ambrogio Buonvicino and Camillo Mariani; the angels' drapery was made of real cloth (cf. Orbaan, 47f.).

22. J. Braun, *Die liturgischen Paramente in Gegenwart und Vergangenheit,* Freiburg-im-Breisgau, 1924, 240; Moroni, *Dizionario,* VI, 57ff.

23. Cf. Siebenhüner, "Umrisse," 309. The height of the bronze columns is given as 45 palmi by G. P. Chattard, *Nuova descrizione del Vaticano . . . ,* Rome, 1762–67, I, 148f. (The Roman palmo was slightly over .22m.)

24. *Tota haec machina ex ligno compacta, subjecto Iconismo expressa ideam exhibebat future molis, quam ex aere, auroque excitare animo inerat Pontificis . . . Nihil tamen Paulo regnante effectum est, sed postquam Urbanus VIII Pontificiae Dignitatis . . .* (Buonanni, *Numismata templi vaticani,* 127, and *Numismata pontificum romanorum,* II, 573)

25. Appendix I Nos. 5–8.

26. See the comments in Appendix I No. 5.

27. In 1618 Grimaldi notes that the pair of spiral columns that had adorned the Oratory of John VII (see n.70 below) *hodie cernuntur ad maiorem templi apsidam pergulam cereorum in pontificijs solemnibus sustinentes caeteris consimilibus saniores, et pulchriores (Opusculum,* fol. 119v).
    In 1635, in a series of notes appended to Grimaldi's treatise, Francesco Speroni, sacristan of Saint Peter's, mentions the number ten: *. . . tempore d.[i] Pontificis* [Paul V] *decem earum integrae delatae fuerunt in novum Templum, ac positae fuerunt ad ornatum ante maiorem apsidem Templi.* (Grimaldi *Opusculum de SS. Veronicae . . .*

of closely related projects of various dates, preserved in drawings and an engraving (Figs. 25–28, 79).[28] These projects are all for ciboria of the ordinary kind, with domes supported on columns. In addition, from the central element they envisage two arms extending outward to the corners of the apse walls, creating a screen-like enclosure before the choir. It is clear that, by reusing the ancient columns, and by screening the apse with an enclosure containing an altar, these designs hark back to the mediaeval arrangement in Saint Peter's, which had remained intact (minus the outer row of columns) until only a decade before the pontificate of Paul V (Fig. 17).[29] The chief difference is that now the ciborium has been fused with the colonnaded screen to form one unit; the result recalls, whether consciously or not, the earliest mediaeval form of the shrine (Fig. 10).

What all these considerations suggest is that the memory of the shrine of Old Saint Peter's was very much alive and that the idea of recreating it in a modern idiom was in force from the time it was dismantled, or at least soon afterward. We shall find that Bernini was motivated by a similar idea. These projects further anticipate that of Bernini in their scale. They would have been some ten meters shorter than Bernini's baldachin (28.97m), but they would have stood in the relatively low choir, not under the main dome.[30]

The two huge models, standing a few meters apart on the axis of Saint Peter's—the baldachin over the tomb and the ciborium in front of the apse—represented opposite poles of tradition; the one was inherently mobile, fragile, and informal, the other was static, permanent, and architectonic. In the development that took place during the next quarter of a century, which culminated in Bernini's baldachin, these two seemingly incompatible traditions were fused.

The crucial link was provided by a third type, intermediate, almost in a literal sense, between the other two. This was the baldachin made usually of perishable materials and suspended in a fixed position above the altar.[31] The type seems to have been introduced into the development of Saint Peter's by Carlo Maderno. At least this is suggested by a rather obscure passage in a manuscript guide to Rome written during the 1660's by Fioravante Martinelli, the friend of Borromini.[32] Martinelli reports that Maderno submitted to Paul V a design that included twisted columns; he adds, however, that the canopy did not actually touch the columns or their cornices. It is difficult to imagine what sort of arrangement was intended, but it is most probable that the canopy was to be sus-

additis aliquibus praecipuis additionibus ad hoc pertinentibus a Francisco Sperono eiusdem Basilicae Sacrista an. D. 1635, Biblioteca Vaticana, MS Vat. lat. 6439, p. 354) Concerning Speroni, see also Pollak, *Die Kunsttätigkeit unter Urban VIII*, 635—henceforth cited as Pollak. (See Addenda and Fig. 28A.)

28. See Appendix I Nos. 18, 20, 23, 26.

29. Cf. the project for rebuilding Saint Peter's by Bernardo Rossellino under Nicolas V in the mid-fifteenth century, as reconstructed by Grimaldi and Martino Ferrabosco (Magnuson, *Roman Quattrocento Architecture*, 177f., 178, fig. 22). A. Schiavo, *San Pietro in Vaticano (Quaderni di Storia dell'arte, IX)*, Rome, 1960, 11, assumes that the twelve columns surrounding the altar in the Grimaldi-Ferrabosco plan were to be the originals.
   We may note, further, a plan for the completion of the church as a whole, ca. 1605–6, which shows an enclosure with an altar flanked by two columns at the entrance to the apse (Fig. 29; Appendix I No. 1); two groups of four columns flank the altar in the crossing. If the ten columns were to be the originals, it would be an early precedent for Bernini's use of spiral columns in the crossing, rather than as a screen in the choir.
   In the other projects it was evidently intended to supplement the preserved originals with copies (cf. Appendix I No. 19).

30. The height of these projects (about 19m) may be judged from the scale (100 palmi) on Borromini's drawing (Fig. 28). The height of Bernini's baldachin is given in P. E. Visconti, *Metrologia vaticana*, Rome, 1828, Table II.

31. Cf. Braun, *Der christ. Altar*, II, 262ff., pls. 187ff.

32. The passage is quoted in its context below, n.53. On Borromini and Martinelli cf. P. Portoghesi, *Borromini nella cultura europea*, Rome, 1964, 96, 200.

pended from above. (A proposal of just this sort was made later, under Urban VIII.[33]) Maderno's project may also have laid the groundwork for one of Bernini's first solutions, in which the canopy, held aloft by angels, was also separate from the columns (cf. Fig. 31, and p. 10 below). The idea of using columns and a canopy is the first evidence of the tendency to combine elements of the traditional baldachin with those of an architectural ciborium.[34]

After the models were built in 1606 there is no further record of construction on the projects during Paul V's lifetime. Effort must have been concentrated on building the nave and the confessio at the tomb; when these were finished the problem came to the fore once more, and new proposals were offered.[35] Before the pope died plans were evidently made to replace the models, perhaps because they had deteriorated in the meantime. However, actual rebuilding of both models, again using temporary materials, began only under Paul V's successor, Gregory XV (1621–1623). The final invoices, which contain detailed descriptions, date from the early years of Urban VIII's pontificate. The description of the apse ciborium given in the painter's invoice corresponds with a project drawn by Borromini, but probably designed by Maderno, which has an inscription bearing the name of Paul V (Fig. 28).[36] The phraseology shows that it was largely a remodeling of the earlier structure, the main alterations being the addition of four straight columns to the ten twisted ones and of four apostles to the cornice of the dome.

Of greater importance are the changes that were introduced in the new baldachin model over the tomb. Payments for the work begin in June, 1622, but it seems possible that a kind of preview of the new model is given in engravings of the great quintuple canonization that took place on March 12 of that year (Figs. 5, 6).[37] The baldachin depicted here is the same basic type as that of Paul V, a tasseled canopy resting on four supports with angels at the bases. There are notable differences, however. The angels, of whom only two are shown, kneel rather than stand, and the supports consist of rich foliate forms. This baldachin may still be Paul V's, again "dressed up" for the ceremony.[38] Yet we shall see presently that the new baldachin, begun within three months after the canonization, also had elaborately carved supports and a new set of angels beside them, executed in

33. Anonymous, *Modo di fare il tabernacolo,* fols. 26r and v; see n.55 below.

34. It is tempting to pair Maderno's project described by Martinelli with one recorded in a drawing by Borromini, but presumably invented by Maderno in 1605–6, for a ciborium with cupola resting on straight columns over the tomb in the crossing (Fig. 14; Appendix I Nos. 2, 17). In this case the relationship—ciborium in the crossing *vs.* baldachin in the choir—would have been the reverse of that of the models. This interchangeability of types is in itself a significant prelude to their fusion.

35. The nave was finished in 1615 (Pastor, xxvi, 394f.). Paul V resolved in Jan., 1611, to build the confessio, which was opened in 1617 (*ibid.,* 401f.; cf. Appendix I No. 9). Papirio Bartoli specifically says that planning for the pontifical choir was delayed by construction of the nave and indecision about the choir's form: ". . . e se bene da molti sommi Pontefici è stato pensato di fare detto Coro [pontificio] . . . con tutto ciò si è restato, sì perche ancora non era finito il corpo della chiesa, sì anco che non si concordava del modo, se bene del luogo la maggior parte concorreva, che si dovesse fare vicino all'Altare de S^{ti} Apostoli . . ." (Bartoli, *Discorso,* int. 1, fol. 1r)

    Projects other than those considered in the text that can securely be dated to the latter part of Paul V's reign are: dismountable choir for the apse recorded in Ferrabosco, *Architettura* (Appendix I No. 22; Appendix II); Papirio Bartoli's proposal for a choir in the form of a navicella to be placed in the crossing and incorporate Maderno's confessio (Fig. 12; Appendix I No. 24); a drawing in the Uffizi attributed to Maderno showing a colonnaded enclosure in the crossing behind the confessio and a choir in the apse (Fig. 13; Appendix I No. 25).

36. Appendix I Nos. 26, 27.

37. Appendix I Nos. 13–15.

38. A record of purchases of material for decorating the baldachin for the canonization is preserved:
Baldachino grande
Per armesino, canne 75 . . . . scudi 337.50
Frangie alte di oro et seta bianca 237.30
Per oro in folio per indorare 104
Per colori, tele, pitura trategi 194

8

stucco by Bernini. Moreover, we shall shortly consider a later canonization print in which Bernini's original design for his bronze baldachin was previewed in just this fashion (cf. Fig. 30). In any case, the baldachin shown in the engravings provides an important link to Bernini's ideas, in that it combines essential elements of both its predecessors. The supports are wholly organic, curvilinear in form, recalling the twisted columns of the ciborium; but they are now used to carry a canopy rather than a cupola. The fact that the angels, in kneeling, seem less actively to carry the structure also implies a significant change in dynamic: the baldachin is thought of as a more self-sufficient, quasi-architectural unit. Two major steps remain in the transition to the final form: the introduction of true columns as supports for the canopy, and the addition of a superstructure.

The new baldachin model as it was actually built is described in the carpenter's final invoice.[39] It too had a fringed canopy, and the supports seem to have incorporated into their regular design something of the ornamentation applied to the earlier structure on special occasions. The ornaments included among other things cherubs, foliage, and spiral fluting.[40] It is not likely that the supports actually had the form of columns, since they are consistently described as staves (aste), and neither capitals nor proper bases are mentioned. But their decoration must in any case have closely resembled that of the ancient spiral shafts, and they thus anticipate Bernini's idea of imitating rather than reusing the originals. It was also intended to gild the supports, which would have given them the effect of being made of metal.[41] Furthermore, the supports were colossal in scale; they stood well over twelve meters high, more than two meters taller than the bronze columns by which Bernini replaced them. A final point of importance is that during the first part of 1624 Bernini himself made four stucco angels for this model; they were apparently placed at the base of the supports, as had been the case previously.[42]

The account book dates from 1615 to 1618, that is, at least four years before the canonization took place; nevertheless there is no hint of any intention to replace the angels.

Cf. I. M. Azzolini, in *Canonizzazione dei santi Ignazio di Loiola*, 127; the account book contains no further references to the baldachin (Rome, Casa Generalizia della Compagnia di Gesù, Archivum Postulationis, Atti concernenti santi, Sez. I, Scaff. A, Busta 16, int. 20).

39. Appendix I No. 13.

40. "Per l'intaglio dele dette 4 Aste alte l'una p¹ 58. con cherubini festoni cartelle cartocci fogliami e scanelate a vite vasi regni mitre colarini e piedi fatto a fogliami." (Pollak, 18 No. 35)

41. The bole and gesso were applied, but the gilding was never carried out (cf. Pollak, 309 No. 1000).

42. He was paid for them between Feb. and Aug., 1624 (Pollak, Nos. 1001ff.). The fact that there were four angels and that the columns had spiral fluting are the chief differences of the model as executed from the baldachin represented in the prints of the canonization of Ignatius of Loyola, *et al.* (Figs. 5, 6). The possibility still remains, however, that the engravings prefigure the intended new baldachin, and that the design was modified in the course of execution (as proved to be the case with Bernini's baldachin). It may also be that the engraver simply omitted the two angels at the back (in one engraving of the canonization of Carlo Borromeo, the rear two angels were omitted, and in another the medallion atop the western face of the canopy was left out; cf. Figs. 2, 3). That the project for the new baldachin was developed during the preparations for the quintuple canonization is suggested by the fact that a preliminary drawing in Vienna for the 1622 prints shows the straight, smooth staves of the earlier structure (Fig. 22; Appendix I No. 11).

Siebenhüner, "Umrisse," 317ff., offers the curious theory that the engraving by Girolamo Frezza in Buonanni, *Num. templ. vat.*, pl. 48, represents the present baldachin, despite the facts that it does not show the carving on the supports mentioned in the documents and that, as is clear from Buonanni's text (p. 127), the plate is based upon Paul V's medal (Fig. 21; Appendix I No. 9).

9

II. Bernini's First Project for the Baldachin

The transition from the baldachin begun under Gregory XV to Urban VIII's enterprise is barely perceptible. The earlier model was never quite finished, and at some point—precisely when is not known—it was decided to return the high altar to its place above the tomb, thus finally reestablishing the predominance of the crossing, but relinquishing the reference to the mediaeval form of the presbytery.[43] We shall see that, paradoxically, the decision may have been at least partly determined by a desire to recreate even more accurately the original form of the shrine. No formal contract with Bernini for the design and construction of a new, permanent structure has been preserved, if one ever existed; payments to him simply began, in July of 1624, while he was still being paid for the stucco angels for the earlier baldachin.[44] The first elements of the new baldachin to be executed were the bronze columns; installation began in September, 1626, and they were unveiled in June of the following year.[45] A separate commission, based on a small model, provided for the superstructure, of which a full-scale model was set in place in April, 1628.[46]

Bernini's first project is recorded, with certain variations, in an engraving showing the decorations he designed for the canonization of Queen Elizabeth of Portugal on March 25, 1625 (Fig. 30),[47] and in medals dated 1626 (Fig. 31) and 1629 (Fig. 32).[48] All three depictions agree on the basic thought underlying the design, which consists of four spiral columns supporting semicircular ribs that intersect diagonally; from the apex, crowning the whole structure, rises a figure of the Resurrected Christ holding the bannered Cross.[49] On the columns are angels who seem to carry the tasseled canopy by means of ribbons strung through loops on its top and secured to the ribs. The representations differ in one important respect. The medal of 1626 shows the canopy raised well above the level of the columns, so that it appears as a completely separate unit. In the engraving of 1625 and the medal of 1629, however, the canopy is lowered to the same height as the capitals and is joined to them by a continuous molding or cornice. This is the solution Bernini adopted in the work finally executed.[50]

---

43. The choir was to be retained in the apse; a model for one was later designed by Bernini (Pollak, 611).
    Bartoli notes in 1620 (*Discorso,* int. 1, fol. 1r) that the choir installations in the apse were temporary and had to be set up and taken down for each occasion; the same is true today.

44. Pollak, Nos. 1053ff.

45. Cf. Pollak, Nos. 1127, 1130.

46. Pollak, Nos. 1142ff., where payments for the large model are wrongly ascribed to the small one; on the installation, see an Avviso of April 8, 1628, quoted in E. Rossi, "Roma ignorata," *Roma,* 15, 1937, 97.

47. Bernini's designs for the canonization were approved by the pope shortly before Feb. 8, 1625 (Fraschetti, *Bernini,* 251 n.1; cf. Pastor, xxix, 10, where the references should be corrected as follows: Bibl. Vat., Arch. Segreto, Acta Consistorialia, Camerarii, xvi, fols. 67v–68, and Bibl. Vat., ms Urb. lat. 1095, fol. 315r, May 28, 1625; Pollak, Nos. 125ff.). The fullest available account of the canonization is that of A. Ribeiro de Vasconcellos, *Evolução do culto de Dona Isabel de Aragão,* Coimbra, 1894, i, 439ff., ii, 190ff. An earlier version of the print (Fig. 23) is discussed in Appendix I No. 12.
    Bernini's canonization installations will be discussed in a separate paper.

48. The medal bearing the date 1626 on the reverse (Fig. 31; Buonanni, *Num. pont.,* ii, 573f., No. xiii) is inscribed with the fourth year of Urban's reign on the obverse, and therefore dates between Sept. 29 (the anniversary of the coronation) and Dec. 31. Both this and a medal of 1633 showing the baldachin in its final form have legends describing the tomb as that of Peter and Paul, reflecting the belief that parts of both apostles' bodies were preserved at Saint Peter's; see n.1 above.
    The medal of 1629 (Fig. 32) honors the canonization of Andrea Corsini in April of that year, for which Bernini also designed the decorations (cf. Pastor, xxix, 9 n.3; Pollak, Nos. 136ff.).

49. In the full-scale model, Christ was to rise from a cloud (Pollak, 354).

50. The drawings by Bernini for the final form of the crown, except for the very latest, show the canopy in the raised position (Brauer-Wittkower, *Zeichnungen,* pls. 6ff.); but the engraving of 1625 and the medal of 1629 indicate that the continuous cornice existed as an alternative solution from the outset.

It is evident that Bernini's project owes a great debt to its predecessors, both visually and conceptually. The idea of using bronze and gilt dates from the time of Paul V, when also it was contemplated to execute a monumental baldachin, rather than a ciborium, over the tomb. The angels and tasseled hangings had appeared in both earlier temporary baldachins. The ciboria with screens planned for the high altar before the apse had incorporated the ancient spiral columns.[51] The notion of imitating the marble shafts in another material may have originated in the previous ciborium and baldachin models. Maderno had thought of using spiral columns with a baldachin, rather than with a dome. The baldachin begun under Gregory XV may have suggested that spiral columns serve as actual supports for the canopy. In several of the earlier projects sculptured figures, including angels, had appeared atop the superstructure (Fig. 34; cf. Figs. 26–28).[52] Finally, the stupendous scale of Bernini's work was by no means an innovation.

Despite this catalogue of precedents, Bernini blends the ingredients in a completely new way. He combines the columns and superstructure proper to a ciborium with the tasseled canopy and supporting angels of a baldachin. His treatment of each of these elements individually, as will become apparent in the following discussion, is equally original. And in the versions that join the canopy directly to the columns he takes the final step in fusing the architectural quality of a permanent ciborium with the transitory quality of a processional baldachin.

Striking confirmation that these were indeed the innovating features of Bernini's design is found in the criticisms voiced against it by certain contemporaries. One of these came from the painter Agostino Ciampelli, and is reported in the manuscript guide to Rome by Fioravante Martinelli, mentioned earlier as the source for our knowledge of Maderno's project.[53] Ciampelli had himself supplied Bernini with a design, but he objected to Bernini's, maintaining that "baldachins are supported not by columns but by staves, and that in any case he would show it borne by angels; and he added that it was a chimera." The objection evidently refers to the solution shown in the engraving of 1625 (Fig. 30) and the medal of 1629 (Fig. 32), in which the columns rather than the angels appear

51. The idea of an independent ciborium with only four spiral columns supporting a cupola occurs in a fresco in the Vatican Library from the time of Sixtus V (1585–90), representing the Council of Ephesus (Fig. 33; A. Taja, *Descrizione del palazzo apostolico vaticano*, 427f.; J. Dupront, "Art et contre-réforme. Les fresques de la Bibliothèque de Sixte-Quint," *MélRome*, 48, 1931, 291). Interestingly enough, there was a tradition that the columns in Saint Peter's had come from a temple of the Ephesian Diana in Greece (Torriggio, *Sacre grotte vaticane*, 283).

52. Appendix I Nos. 16, 18, 26.

53. F. Martinelli, *Roma ornata dall'architettura, pittura, e scoltura*, Rome, Bibl. Casanatense, MS 4984, p. 201:
   Fù pensiero di Paolo V coprire con baldacchino l'altar maggiore di S. Pietro con ricchezza proportionata all'apertura fatta alla confessione e sepolcro dl d.º Onde Carlo Maderno gli presentò un disegno con colonne à vite; ma il baldacchino non toccava le colonne, ne il lor cornicione: sopragionse la morte di Pauolo, e restò l'op.a sul disegno sin al ponteficato di Urbano VIII. il quale disse al d.º Carlo si contentasse, che il Bernino facesse d.ª opera. Il Cavalier Celio, forse non ben informato del tutto, stampò essere inventione di Santiss.º giuditio (cioè del Papa) messo in opera dal d.º Bernino. Vincenzo Berti manoscritto appresso Mons.ʳ Landucci Sacrista di N'ro Sig.ʳᵉ Alessandro VII. e p le sue eminenti virtudi dignissimo di grado superiore, ha scritto, esser disegno del Ciampelli cognato del d.º Bernini, il che non sò se sia vero; ma si bene non concorreva con d.º Bernini circa l'abbigliam.ᵗⁱ et altro; e diceva, che li Baldacchini non si sostengono con le colonne, ma con l'haste, e che in ogni modo voleva mostrare che lo reggono li Angeli: e soggiongeva che era una chimera.
   The passage occurs as a marginal correction to the original text, which is canceled but can be deciphered: "Il Ciborio con colonne di metallo istorte à vite dell'altar maggiore è disegno del Cav. Bernino, et il getto è di Gregorio de Rossi Rom.º Ma il Cav.ʳᵉ Celio scrive essere inventione di santissimo giuditio messo in opera dal d.º Cav.ʳᵉ Vincenzo Berti manoscritto appresso monsig.ʳᵉ Landucci sacrista di N. S.ʳᵉ hà lasciato scritto esser disegno del Ciampelli cognato di d.º Bernino." (See Addenda.)
   The reference from Celio's guidebook concerning Urban VIII's contribution is as follows: "L'altare maggiore con le colonne fatte à vite e suoi aderenti, il tutto di metallo indorato, Inventione di santissimo giuditio, messo in opera dal Cavalier Lorenzo Bernino." (*Memoria fatta dal Signor Gaspare Celio . . . delli nomi dell'artefici delle pitture, che sono in alcune chiese . . . di Roma*, Naples, 1638, 70) The publisher of this work, Scipione Bonino, writes in the introduction (pp. 4f.) that it was based on a manuscript of Celio's written in 1620, and that almost all the additional information about works done since then came from Sebastiano Vannini, "Galeno di questi

to be the chief support of the canopy; this was a grave breach of architectural etiquette, and the result is truly a hybrid, chimerical form.[54] To another, anonymous writer who submitted an alternative project of his own, the superstructure appeared unworkable. He claimed that "an open arch could not possibly support a figure, and also hold together columns of such great weight."[55] This argument seems to have weighed heavily in the ultimate decision to substitute a cross and globe for the Risen Christ and to increase the number and change the shape of the ribs (see p. 23 below).

From an aesthetic point of view the key to Bernini's solution lay in the idea of discarding the ancient spiral columns themselves, and instead imitating them on a larger scale. What he achieved may best be understood by comparing his project with the earlier ones for screen-ciboria in the choir, which were to reuse the ancient shafts (Figs. 26–28, 79). The original columns were dwarfed by the new building, and to gain height the earlier projects included both an attic and a drum between the capitals and the dome; the resulting vertical accent was safely counterbalanced by the lateral wings. For a structure in the crossing even more height was needed, but the wings were an obstruction and had to be removed.[56] By enlarging the columns Bernini was able to omit the drum and attic, and thus create a more balanced proportion without the help of the wings. It might be said that Bernini's solution made it aesthetically possible to keep the high altar and tomb together in the crossing. It also made possible the fusion of baldachin and ciborium types, for in the absence of both drum and attic Bernini could rest the superstructure directly on the columns and cover the intervening space with a fringed canopy.

The design of the crown itself serves a dual function, in keeping with the nature of the whole conception. Its domical shape suggests the cupolas with which ordinary ciboria were often covered, while its open ribs deny the sense of weight and mass that a cupola normally conveys. The perfo-

tempi." Vannini was the author, among other things, of two poems to Fioravante Martinelli (Bibl. Vat., MS Barb. lat. 2109, fols. 162f.). Baglione describes Celio's book as "pieno d'errori" (Baglione, *Vite*, 381).

The source of the story is probably a passage in a manuscript dialogue by Lelio Guidiccioni (kindly brought to my attention by Cesare D'Onofrio), in which Guidiccioni (*L.*) and Bernini (*G.L.*) are the conversants. The context of the passage is an elaborate eulogy of Urban VIII's expertise in artistic matters; Bernini asks, "Di chi pensate, che sia il pensiero dell'Altar Vaticano, tale, quale sia divenuta l'opera? *L.* Vostro hò sempre pensato. *G.L.* À pensarla meglio, dite di S. Sta *L.* Dunque voi sete pure obietto di lode sua; la quale è origine della vostra . . ." (Bibl. Vat., MS Barb. lat. 3879, fol. 53v) The dialogue is datable to Sept., 1633, since it contains a reference (fol. 51v) to the death within the last days of Antonio Querengo (d. Sept. 1, 1633; G. Vedova, *Biografia degli scrittori padovani*, Padua, 1832–36, II, 134f.). It is conceivable that the phrase "quale sia divenuta l'opera" refers to the decision to change the superstructure. (See now C. D'Onofrio, "Un dialogo-recita di Gianlorenzo Bernini," *Palatino*, 10, 1966, 127ff.)

Except for two letters, dated 1660, in the Biblioteca Nazionale, Florence (c.v.90.147; c.v.97.5), I have been unable to identify the Vincenzo Berti whose manuscript is mentioned as the source of the story about Agostino Ciampelli. Ambrogio Landucci was a well-known Augustinian, a native of Siena (D. A. Perini, *Bibliografia agostiniana*, Florence, 1929–38, I, 143ff.), for whom Borromini designed an altar (H. Thelen, *Istituto austriaco di cultura in Roma. 70 Disegni di Francesco Borromini* [Exhibition Catalogue], Rome, 1958, 24 No. 54). He died in Rome on Feb. 16, 1669, leaving his books and manuscripts to the Convent of San Martino in Siena. His testament is accompanied by an inventory of his library which includes 121 items, but they are listed with short titles only and none is identifiable as the one by Berti that Martinelli mentions (Rome, Arch. di Stato, Notaio Bellisarius, Busta 243, fols. 465v, 535ff.). The library of San Martino passed to the Biblioteca Comunale of Siena, whose director kindly informs me that an inventory of the convent's library contains the following entry: *Berti Quaestiones regulares.* But no manuscript answering the description appears in L. Ilari, *Indice per materie della Biblioteca Comunale di Siena*, 7 vols., Siena, 1844–51.

The statement that Ciampelli and Bernini were brothers-in-law cannot be strictly true. Ciampelli—who died not in 1642, as is commonly reported, but on April 22, 1630 (Rome, Arch. del. Vicariato, San Giovanni dei Fiorentini, *Liber Defunctorum* 1626–1716, fol. 16r)—was married to a woman named Camilla Latina (*ibid.*, S. Giov. Fior., *Liber Baptizatorum* 1616–49, fol. 82v), who did not remarry after Ciampelli's death, while Bernini married Caterina Tezio in 1639 (Fraschetti, *Bernini*, 104f.).

We may note, finally, a drawing by Ciampelli with twisted columns mentioned in an inventory of Cardinal Francesco Barberini: "Una carta fattoci in penna l'Anuntiata dipinta con diverse Colori e due Colòne ritorte di mano di Agostino Ciampelli, alta p.^{mi} uno e larga tre quarti di palmo." (Bibl. Vat., Arch. Barberini, Arm. 155, *Inventario di tutte le robbe . . . nel Palazzo della Cancellaria del . . . Card.^{le} Fran.^{co} Barberino*, Oct., 1649, p. 68)

54. Since Ciampelli died early in 1630 (see the previous footnote) he presumably did not know the final version, which was not worked out until 1631 (see p. 23 below).

Criticism of Bernini's architectural "grammar" seems implicit also in Teodoro della Porta's offer to submit a

rated superstructure recalls a common mediaeval type of ciborium, in which one or more orders of colonnettes resting on the main entablature act as a kind of drum for the dome.[57] Bernini's open ribs had been anticipated in a ciborium by Giovanni Caccini in Santo Spirito in Florence, where open metal strapwork screens the space between the thin ribs of an octagonal cupola (Fig. 36).[58] But while this tradition may have paved the way for Bernini's general conception, his design has its most precise antecedent in the central portion of the shrine built over the apostle's tomb by Constantine in the early fourth century (Fig. 10). There, four of the twisted columns also supported semicircular intersecting ribs.

Though careful records were kept of the excavations beneath the crossing when the foundations for the bronze columns were dug, it is improbable that these could have yielded such accurate information concerning the elevation of the Constantinian shrine.[59] Rather, the source of Bernini's astonishing piece of archaeological reconstruction seems to have been a unique medal, now lost, of the early Christian period (Fig. 38). On one side a tabernacle appears that has been regarded as a depiction of the shrine in Saint Peter's.[60] It consists of four twisted columns surmounted by two semicircular arches placed diagonally, exactly the form that can be reconstructed, on independent grounds, for the main feature of the early mediaeval confessio of Saint Peter's. The similarity of Bernini's design to that on the medal extends even to the swags of drapery hung between the columns and to the interposition of a continuous cornice between columns and open crown.

Precisely how Bernini came to know the medal cannot be determined, but its history has been traced to within a decade of his project; it was given to the pope's nephew Cardinal Francesco Barberini in March, 1636, by Claude Ménétrier, the French antiquarian living in Rome.[61] Ménétrier,

project according to the good rules of architecture (Appendix I No. 28ʙ); this is perhaps to be identified with a drawing in the Albertina (Fig. 35; Appendix I No. 28c).

55. *Modo di fare il tabernacolo,* fol. 26r: ". . . e non puol mai un Archetto in aria sostenere ne figura ne unite le colonne di tanto gravissimo peso, come il Cavaliere hà esposto, che essendo di gettito oltre la grossa spesa non necessaria è pericolosa di motivo di gran rovina."
   The project was to be executed in bronze and copper over a wooden core and use columns decorated with bees, laurel, and animals to support an architrave, upon which eight putti were placed, "fingendo di portare come per Aria il Baldachino che sarà attaccato nella volta di sopra con Ingegno di poterlo levare" (*ibid.*); the idea seems to recall the project of Carlo Maderno, reported by Fioravante Martinelli (pp. 7f. above).

56. Ferrabosco's project with wings was rejected by Urban VIII because it occupied too much space (see n.179 below).

57. Braun, *Der christ. Altar,* ɪɪ, pls. 160ff.

58. Designed by 1599, dedicated in 1608 (cf. W. and E. Paatz, *Die Kirchen von Florenz,* Frankfurt-am-Main, 1940–54, v, 140f.).
   A few years later Bernini drew even closer to Caccini's ciborium, in the catafalque he designed for the funeral of the pope's brother Carlo Barberini (d. 1630), known from a workshop drawing in Windsor (Fig. 37). Here he used a proper open-ribbed dome, crowning it with a figure of death analogous to the Risen Christ on the baldachin (cf. Brauer-Wittkower, *Zeichnungen,* 162 n.6; A. Blunt and H. L. Cooke, *The Roman Drawings of the XVII and XVIII Centuries in the Collection of Her Majesty the Queen at Windsor Castle,* London, 1960, 25 No. 48; No. 49, Inv. No. 5612, seems to have no connection with the Barberini catafalque). The catafalque is discussed in an unpublished doctoral dissertation by O. Berendsen, "Italian Sixteenth and Seventeenth Century Catafalques," New York University, 1961, 132f., fig. 48. A ground plan study for the catafalque by Borromini is in Vienna, Albertina, Architektonische Handzeichnungen, Rom, Kirchen, No. 64; 214 x 173mm.

59. See the accounts of the excavations published in Armellini, *Le chiese di Roma,* ɪɪ, 862ff., and H. Lietzmann, *Petrus und Paulus in Rom,* Berlin-Leipzig, 1927, 194ff., 304ff. An attempt under Urban VIII to reconstruct the confessio in detail from literary sources is noted below, p. 14.

60. Cf. most recently F. Castagnoli, "Probabili raffigurazioni del ciborio intorno alla memoria di S. Pietro in due medaglie del IV secolo," *Rivista di archeologia cristiana,* 29, 1953, 98ff.; A. Baird, "La colonna santa," *BurlM,* 24, 1913–14, 128ff. A badly oxidized lead cast of the medal was preserved in the Museo Sacro of the Vatican, the original bronze having been lost; the cast has since also disappeared, perhaps oxidized into unrecognizability. (See Addenda.)

61. See the brilliant piece of research tracing the medal's history by G. B. De Rossi, "Le medaglie di devozione dei primi sei o sette secoli della chiesa," *B di archeologia cristiana,* 7, 1869, 33ff.
   "Vous treuverez . . . un soulphre que j'ay jetté sur une petite lame de metal Corinthe de cave laquelle j'achepta ces jours passés et donna à Monseig.ʳ l'Ecc. Card.ˡᵉ Pat.ⁿᵉ, lequel tesmogna luy plaire grandement pour estre une pièce de la primitive Eglise." (Letter of Ménétrier to Nicolas Peiresc, March 8, 1636; *ibid.,* 35)

who sent a cast of the medal to his colleague Nicolas Peiresc in Paris to get the latter's interpretation, does not say when or where the medal was discovered, or from whom it was acquired. But he reports that it had been found together with a representation in gold glass of Sts. Peter and Paul—a circumstance that, especially in view of the legend linking the bodies of the two apostles, must have reinforced the association with Saint Peter's suggested inevitably by the twisted columns. The medal's testimony must have been further supported by a passage in Gregory of Tours (538–594), who reports that over the tomb was a ciborium resting on four white columns; in a learned treatise on the ancient confessio, submitted to Urban VIII before Bernini's baldachin was built, the passage is taken as an accurate description of the original monument.[62] If the medal was believed to show the shrine in its pristine form—that is, as an independent structure without wings—knowledge of it may even have influenced the basic decision to return the high altar to its place over the tomb in the crossing.

This clear and deliberate effort to recreate the early Christian monument while retaining essential elements from the recent predecessors may be what chiefly distinguishes Bernini's work as a new departure. But the motivation was more than simply one of archaeological exactitude, as becomes evident when one considers the baldachin's meaning.

Of the twelve white spiral columns that decorated the mediaeval presbytery, eleven are still preserved.[63] Eight were installed by Bernini in the upper reliquary niches in the crossing piers (Figs. 53–56; see p. 21 below), one is the Colonna Santa referred to earlier (p. 3 above), and two flank the altar presently dedicated to St. Francis in the Chapel of the Holy Sacrament off the north aisle of the basilica (Fig. 39). These columns were the subject of various legends, by far the most widespread of which was that they had been brought by Constantine from the Temple of Solomon at Jerusalem. The association was so strong that twisted columns were often used by artists in representations of the Temple (Fig. 40),[64] and the allusion to the Holy City is implicit in the columns of Bernini's baldachin as well. In fact, even apart from the spiral columns, parallels between Saint Peter's and the Temple in layout, measurement, and decoration were long thought to exist.[65] One in particular

62. Michele Lonigo, "Breve relatione del Sito, qualità, e forma antica della Confessione . . ." in Buonanni, *Num. templ. vat.*, 191ff. (cf. p. 198); Buonanni says (p. 115) that Lonigo, who was papal archivist and master of ceremonies under Paul V, submitted the work to Urban VIII before the baldachin was built. The essential passage in Gregory of Tours is: *Sunt ibi et columnae mirae elegantiae candore niveo quattuor numero, quae ciborium sepulchri sustinere dicuntur.* (*De gloria beatorum martyrum* 28, *PL*, LXXI, 729)

63. On the columns see especially J. B. Ward Perkins, "The Shrine of St. Peter and its Twelve Spiral Columns," *JRS*, 42, 1952, 21ff., and Alfarano, *De basil. vat.*, 53ff.

64. Some further examples are mentioned in nn.67, 107 below.

65. The relationship was already explicit in Nicolas V's project for rebuilding Saint Peter's (cf. Magnuson, *Roman Quattrocento Architecture*, 210, 360–62), and according to L. D. Ettlinger it is reflected in the early decoration of the Sistine Chapel (*The Sistine Chapel*, 79f.). For the sixteenth century, see the many references in Alfarano, *De basil. vat.*, 221, s.v. "Templum Salomonis."

66. *Haud aliter quidem Constantinus Imperator et Beatus Silvester Papa circa beati Petri Apostoli Corpus et Altare fecerunt quam Moses et Aaron fecerant circa Arcam foederis Domini tabulas legis et urnam continentem, quam Dei monitu in Tabernaculi medio intra sancta sanctorum sub cherubim alas constituerant. Et Salomon in Templo Domini idem fecerat.* (Alfarano, *De basil. vat.*, 29) The allusion is to Hebrews 9:3–5. (See Addenda.)

67. I Kings 7:21; II Chron. 3:17. Cf. S. Yeivin, "Jachin and Boaz," *Palestine Exploration Quarterly*, 1959, 6ff.
   In a painting of the Presentation of the Virgin by Domenichino in Savona (Borea, *Domenichino*, pl. 78) and in a miniature of the Marriage of the Virgin in the Book of Hours of Etienne Chevalier by Jean Fouquet (K. Perls, *Jean Fouquet*, London-Paris-New York, 1940, 53), the entrance to the Temple is actually shown flanked by a pair of the spiral columns of Saint Peter's; in the Fouquet the columns are tinted to imitate gilt metal.
   I am convinced that Bernini later had in mind a dual reference to Old Saint Peter's and Jerusalem when he included the window with the dove of the Holy Spirit above the Cathedra Petri in the west apse; Alfarano speaks of the setting sun penetrating the rear windows of the old basilica: *ad occasum tendens per posteriores Basilicae fenestras dictam Aram maximam, totamque Basilicam irradiat sicut Arcam Foederis intra sancta sanctorum Tabernaculi Mosi et Salomonis Templi existentem per anteriores portas ingrediens olim illustrabat.* (*De basil. vat.*, 19) It should be recalled that the orientation of Saint Peter's is unusual in that the apse is to the west.

68. Ward Perkins, "The Shrine of St. Peter," 26, 32, was evidently the first to observe that two of the columns had been cut down, and that these in particular served as Bernini's model for the baldachin.

14

is important here, since it involves specifically the Temple and St. Peter's tomb. It is stated by Tiberio Alfarano (d. 1596), who was a cleric of Saint Peter's, in his description of the old basilica: "The emperor Constantine and Pope Sylvester did no differently about the body and altar of the apostle Peter than Moses and Aaron had done about the Ark of the Covenant containing the tablets of the Law and the urn, which at God's command they constructed in the center of the Tabernacle inside the Holy of Holies under the wings of cherubim. And Solomon did the same in the Temple of the Lord."[66] The cherubim mentioned here seem to find an echo in the angels who spread their wings above Bernini's baldachin; indeed this may well have been among the reasons for shifting them from beside the supports, their position in the previous baldachins, to the top. It is even possible that the very material of the baldachin was intended to carry out this theme, recalling the famous pair of brazen columns with which Solomon had flanked the Tabernacle.[67]

To be sure, the allusion to the Temple was already implicit in the reuse of the ancient columns in earlier projects. But it is important to emphasize that Bernini's bronze columns differ from the originals in several ways. The enveloping vine tendrils of the originals have been transformed by Bernini into laurel, a Barberini device that occurs throughout the crossing along with the pope's famous bees and sun. In making this change, an essential symbolic element of the columns—the age-old association of the vine scroll with the Christian sacrament—was lost. Yet there seems to have been an allusion to the sacrament in the form Bernini gave to the columns. He did not imitate the normal type, with alternating bands of fluting and foliage (cf. Figs. 53–56). Rather, he singled out those which, evidently as a result of having been shortened at some time, have fluting only on the lower portions.[68] Two columns of precisely this form had been used by Paul III in the mid-sixteenth century to decorate the altar of the Holy Sacrament in the old nave (Fig. 41).[69] Their subsequent history is uncertain, but it is surely significant that Bernini used two of the same type, perhaps the same pair, to flank the lateral altar in the Chapel of the Holy Sacrament in the new church (Fig. 39).[70] The cycle of interrelationships is carried out also in the stucco scene in the vault of the chapel

69. Alfarano, *De basil. vat.*, 55, 63f.

70. The altar, then dedicated to St. Maurice, was decorated from April, 1636 (Pollak, Nos. 890ff.). The chapel as a whole was first intended as a sacristy; the request of the Archconfraternity of the Sacrament to have it assigned to them was approved in 1626 (Pollak, No. 872).

   Grimaldi in fact shows four columns of this type, two of them on the old sacrament altar (Fig. 41) and two flanking the entrance to the Chapel of John VII (705–7), which was located at the Porta Santa. Grimaldi (quoted n.27 above) says that in his day the columns of the John VII monument were to be seen before the main apse, along with other similar columns, making no mention of what happened to the pair from the sacrament altar. Both Cerrati and Ward Perkins assume that the pair now in the Chapel of the Holy Sacrament came from the John VII chapel. But Ward Perkins seems to have overlooked the sacrament altar of Paul III altogether, while Cerrati (ed. of Alfarano, *De basil. vat.*, 55, 106 n.2) seems not to have noticed that the extant pair have been altered and assumed that they were copies; except for minor restored details, they are certainly antique. The problems would be resolved if Schüller-Piroli is right in stating (I know not on what evidence) that the same pair was simply shifted from the John VII chapel to the sacrament altar in old Saint Peter's (*2000 Jahre Sankt Peter*, Olten, 1950, 629). They would subsequently have been moved to the apse of the new basilica, where Grimaldi saw them, and finally to the Chapel of the Sacrament. A drawing in Berlin attributed to Etienne Dupérac shows the Colonna Santa beside a row of four columns of the "sacramental" type, without any architectural setting; M. Winner assumes that Dupérac invented two of the sacramental columns (*Zeichner sehen die Antike. Europäische Handzeichnungen 1450–1800* [Exhib. Cat.], Berlin-Dahlem, 1967, 129f. No. 80, pl. 48).

   There has also been considerable confusion about the fate of the missing column or columns. Cerrati believes that three columns were lost or destroyed in transport; others, accepting the pair in the sacrament chapel as originals, have theorized that one column was given away (cf. Cerrati, in Alfarano, *De basil. vat.*, 55). A possible answer to this problem is suggested by the sacrament columns themselves. Though at some time the intermediate zone of fluting was removed, their actual height is precisely the same as the rest of the series (that is, 4.70m, as reported by Cerrati, *ibid.*, 55; the figure 3.60m, given in the caption to Ward Perkins' pl. v fig. 1, is erroneous). Furthermore, this pair of columns is different from all the others in several respects, notably in that the vine scrolls are inhabited only by birds and other animals; there are no putti. What all this suggests is that the missing

15

directly above this altar (Fig. 40).[71] The panel shows Solomon examining the plans of the Temple of Jerusalem; in the background is a complex structure in course of construction, which includes four columns of this same design.[72] Equally striking, the columns of the Temple support an inward curving entablature, a device that in the final version Bernini applied to the sides of the baldachin (cf. Fig. 43).

The allusion to the sacrament in Bernini's first project for the baldachin is far more pervasive than the choice of the columns alone would suggest. Around 1600 Clement VIII had erected a great altar of the sacrament at the Lateran. This Constantinian foundation—the cathedral of Rome and the mother church of Catholicism, at whose high altar, as at Saint Peter's, only the pope may officiate —had been lavishly restored by Clement. He had decorated the confessio before the papal altar, which is mentioned in a document as one of the models for Paul V's confessio at Saint Peter's.[73] Under the direction of the Cavaliere d'Arpino the upper part of the lateral transept walls had been covered with a series of frescoes illustrating the life of Constantine. On the end of the south transept wing, D'Arpino painted a grandiose fresco of the Ascension of Christ. Below this is the Altar of the Sacrament, designed by Pier Paolo Olivieri as a wall tabernacle in the form of a temple front (Fig. 42). Four colossal bronze columns support the triangular pediment, which is also of gilt metal. Here the idea of a monumental tabernacle all in bronze had actually been realized.

Its relevance for the Saint Peter's altar was more than a matter of scale and material. The bronze columns of the Lateran were also the subject of various legends, among the current ones being that they too had once adorned the Temple at Jerusalem, whence they had been brought by the Empress Helen.[74] They thus embodied the same allusion as the spiral columns of Saint Peter's and provided an additional motive for using bronze. The back of the Lateran altar was ornamented with a relief of the Last Supper in solid silver, which served as a reliquary cover for a portion of cedar wood believed to have come from the table at which Christ and the disciples supped; the relief was melted down in the eighteenth century during the French occupation of Rome (and later replaced). But the sacramental nature of the altar was also provided by another relic: the columns were supposed to be filled with earth from Mount Calvary upon which Christ shed his blood at the Crucifixion, again brought back to Rome by Helen. This lent a real, topographical basis to the allusion to Jerusalem, and we shall later consider another exactly parallel case that was directly pertinent to Saint Peter's.

twelfth column may have been of the same unusual type as the sacrament pair and that it was cut up and portions used to bring the latter two back to their original length. When these operations might have taken place is impossible to say. A payment of June, 1637, when the altar in the sacrament chapel was readied, records the addition of a piece to one of the columns (Pollak, 277 No. 897); but this probably refers to the bottom half of the lowest ring of acanthus on the left-hand column.

It should be noted finally that a sixteenth century engraving of one of the sacrament columns appears in various versions of A. Lafréry's *Speculum Romanae magnificentiae* (e.g., Bibl. Vat., Riserva S. 6. fol. 18, with title page dated 1587); doubtless this was the print mistakenly identified as representing the Colonna Santa in the 1572 list of Lafréry's prints published by F. Ehrle, *Roma prima di Sisto V. La pianta di Roma Du Pérac-Lafréry del 1577*, Rome, 1908, 55 (cf. Cerrati, in Alfarano, *De basil. vat.*, 55). The print seems to show the column in its shortened state.

71. Payments to Giovanni Battista Ricci for the cartoons for the narrative stucco panels in the choir began in May, 1621 (Rome, Arch. della Rev. Fabbrica di S. Pietro, I Piano, Ser. 1, Vol. 246, *Spese* 1621–23, fol. 17r); the sacristy is first mentioned in the payments in Dec., 1622 (*ibid.*, fol. 72v). His payments ended in Dec., 1626 (Pollak, Nos. 705ff.; cf. No. 33). The areas surrounding the narratives had been designed earlier by Ferrabosco (Beltrami, "Ferabosco," 30). The execution extended into the reign of Urban VIII (Pollak, Nos. 712ff., Feb., 1623–Aug., 1627).

72. These columns had often been imitated, but I would mention one instance in Rome in which the sacramental association seems evident; namely, in the Oratorio del Gonfalone, where they form the general framework of the fresco cycle (1568–84) illustrating the Passion (cf. A. Molfino, *L'oratorio del Gonfalone*, Rome, 1964). Here they also appear prominently in the background of Livio Agresti's *Last Supper* (*ibid.*, fig. 22). A chapel in Santo Spirito in Sassia with frescoes by Agresti (Fig. 57; see p. 22 below) seems to have provided the model for Bernini's own use of the columns in the upper niches of the piers in Saint Peter's.

The Lateran altar, in keeping with its dedication to the sacrament, has the Trinity as its overall theme (cf. Fig. 45). God the Father is depicted in the triangular opening of the pediment, while on the underside of the roof appears the dove of the Holy Ghost. Combined with the crucifix on the altar itself, these form the three elements of the traditional formula for representing the Trinity, in their usual vertical sequence. The same elements are distributed in an analogous way at Saint Peter's. The dove is also shown on the underside of the baldachin's canopy above the altar crucifix, while God the Father appears in the lantern at the apex of the dome (Fig. 43).[75] The latter figure was executed when the decoration of the dome began, also directed by the Cavaliere d'Arpino, under Clement VIII.[76]

A similar arrangement had occurred in the Church of Santa Maria dei Monti in Rome, designed by Giacomo della Porta and built and decorated after 1580 (Fig. 44).[77] Here the high altar, with its famous miraculous image of the Virgin, also holds the tabernacle containing the Eucharist. The dove of the Holy Spirit appears in the conch of the apse above the altar (also in the stucco decoration around the base of the drum), and God the Father is depicted in the lantern of the dome. The special emphasis given to the sacrament in the Madonna dei Monti may be explained by the fact that it was the church of the Confraternity of the Catechumens, whose purpose was to instruct and assist Jews and other non-believers wishing to convert to Catholicism.[78]

All these considerations shed light upon what would surely have been one of the most spectacular features of Bernini's baldachin, the great figure of the Resurrected Christ at the center of the crown in the first project.[79] Monumental altar ciboria are most frequently surmounted by the cross and globe (Figs. 14, 18, 24, etc.), and so eventually was Bernini's baldachin. Instead, Bernini's use of the Risen Saviour in the first project recalls the eucharistic images—in which Christ is shown usually with a chalice and holding a cross—that often occur on tabernacles intended to hold the sacrament (Fig. 45).[80] Yet Bernini's Christ held the banner associated with the Resurrection as a narrative event rather than a symbolic type, and there was no chalice; this is exactly the sort of figure that occurs in the Lateran sacrament altar, on a small scale in bronze atop the cupola of the lavishly decorated altar tabernacle (Fig. 46), and in a life-size marble surmounting the high altar in Santa Maria dei Monti (Fig. 44).

73. "La Santità di Nostro Signore . . . risolvè di far aprire sotto l'altar maggiore di San Pietro . . . in quella guisa, che stanno le cappelle sotto l'altar maggiore di San Giovanni Laterano et del Presepio in Santa Maria Maggiore." (Avviso of Jan. 26, 1611, in Orbaan, 98)
   For Clement VIII's work at the Lateran, see Pastor, XXIV, 475ff.

74. On the legends concerning the Lateran columns, cf. Panciroli, *Tesori nascosti*, 139f.; Severano, *Memorie sacre*, I, 506f.; C. Rasponi, *De basilica et patriarchio lateranensi*, Rome, 1657, 32, 47f.

75. H. Sedlmayr has also emphasized the relation of the baldachin to the dome mosaics in Saint Peter's and, though in a different way, has seen the reference to the Trinity (*Epochen und Werke*, Vienna, 1960, II, 23ff.).
   In Paul V's baldachin, as the medal of 1617 shows (Fig. 21), the underside of the canopy was covered with stars.

76. On the chronology of the dome decorations, cf. Siebenhüner, "Umrisse," 300.

77. Cf. Pastor, XX, 583.

78. See Moroni, *Dizionario*, XLVII, 270ff.

79. It may be relevant that images of the Resurrected Christ had appeared on coins struck during the *sede vacante* of 1623, the period between the death of Gregory XV and the election of Urban; the obverses bear the arms of Cardinal Ippolito Aldobrandini, nephew of Clement VIII, who was Camerlengo. But these have no known connection with the basilica. Cf. E. Martinori, *Annali della Zecca di Roma. Sede vacante 1621 . . .* , Rome, 1919, 17ff.; *Corpus nummorum italicorum*, Milan, 1910ff., XVI, 269ff.

80. A. Marquand, *Luca della Robbia*, Princeton, 1914, 61ff., considers the door in the Peretola tabernacle to be a later insertion; in any case, the figure of Christ follows the traditional eucharistic type. Cf. also Braun, *Der christ. Altar*, II, pls. 346 left, 348, 350 left.

Thus, the substitution of the Risen Christ for the usual cross and globe, in conjunction with the Trinity, embodies a reference to the sacrament; and the form these elements were given seems to derive specifically from two of the most recent and conspicuous altars in Rome that held the sacrament.

It should be noted, finally, that reflections of the Lateran sacrament altar are found in Bernini's work long after the baldachin was completed. The general organization of the altar at the end of the transept served as a model for his Chapel of Saint Teresa in the transept of Santa Maria della Vittoria (begun 1647). There is also evidence that the relief of the Last Supper on the altar frontal of the Teresa chapel may have been based specifically on the lost silver relief of the Lateran altar.[81] Toward the end of his life he placed a figure of the Resurrected Christ without a chalice atop the cupola of the sacrament altar he himself designed for Saint Peter's (1670's).[82]

The reference to the sacrament is only part of the significance of the figure on the baldachin. The decoration of the dome of Saint Peter's had been completed under Paul V. Around its base the twelve apostles had been depicted, with Christ enthroned and flanked by the Virgin and John the Baptist in the west side facing the nave; in the compartments above, angels hold the instruments of the Passion (Fig. 47). The scheme is familiar from depictions of the Last Judgment, and the figure atop the baldachin was certainly conceived in this context. The basic imagery of the crossing would have comprised the sacrifice at the altar and, above, Christ rising from the tomb to assume his place in heaven as King and Judge.[83] The Christ figure thus charges the physical space of the crossing with the meaning of a dramatic action; we are actually at Jerusalem and salvation is being achieved before our very eyes.

The conception of the baldachin that emerges from these considerations may be summarized under three headings: historical, liturgical, and geographical. Historically, through its paraphrase of the ancient spiral columns and its basic design, it recalls the original monument in Saint Peter's. Liturgically, through the design of the columns and the figure of Christ, it refers to the Holy Sacrament. And geographically, the Risen Christ, the spiral columns, and perhaps even the use of bronze, involve a reference to Jerusalem, the site of Christian redemption. This imagery became fundamental to Bernini's treatment of the crossing as a whole.

81. I have in preparation a monograph on the Saint Teresa chapel, in which the relations to the Lateran altar will be discussed. Bernini's *Last Supper* is illustrated in E. Lavagnino, *et al., Altari barocchi in Roma*, Rome, 1959, pl. on p. 83. As far as I can discover the connection is first mentioned in A. Nibby, *Roma nell'anno MDCCCXXXVIII*, Rome, 1838–41, Moderna, I, 530, but there is good reason to believe it is true; in the engraving of the Lateran altar in the series by Giovanni Maggi discussed in Appendix I No. 8, the relief is shown with a composition very close to Bernini's. A similar composition is also shown in a medal commemorating the altar (Buonanni, *Num. pont.*, II, 457 fig. XI, but the engraving here is inaccurate; see instead A. Ciaconius, *Vitae, et res gestae pontificum romanorum . . .* , Rome, 1677, IV, cols. 275f., No. 17; examples of the medal are preserved in the Staatliche Münzsammlung, Munich, and in the Bibliothèque Nationale, Paris).

82. Visible in the illustration in Fraschetti, *Bernini*, 395. No banner is attached to the cross-staff held by Christ in the work as we know it; but it is interesting to note that a banner does appear in a drawing at Windsor with projects for adding candelabra, which Brauer and Wittkower believe was made after the altar was finished (*Zeichnungen*, 173, 175, pl. 195c). The Christ on the Saint Peter's ciborium rises from a cloud, as did the figure in the first version of the baldachin (see n.49 above).

   For the relationship between the Lateran sacrament altar and the crossing of Saint Peter's as a whole, see n.164 below.

83. This theme also seems embodied in the ornaments of the upper reliquary niches of the piers; symbols of the Passion appear in the lower part of the frontispieces, symbols of salvation above (see nn.121, 164 below). An element of vertical integration involving the building itself was also present at the Lateran, with the crucifix on the altar, the Resurrected Christ on the ciborium, and the Ascension of Christ on the wall above the tabernacle.

III. The Decoration of the Pier Niches

Planning for the four piers and their decoration began when it was still expected to execute the baldachin according to Bernini's first project. Urban had already shown his concern for the condition of the relics when in January, 1624, he ordered a complete reconstruction of the reliquary niche for the Holy Face and the Lance; it was finished late in the following year.[84] The crucial decision to redecorate the lower niches beneath the relics must have been taken shortly thereafter. This is evident from a document in the archive of the basilica reported by Baldinucci in the famous defense of Bernini's work on the piers, which he appended to his biography of the artist; the document shows that two models for altars, "uno sotto al nicchio del Volto Santo e l'altro di S. Andrea," were in existence by June of 1626.[85] During the first part of 1627 payments were made for a group of models for the Veronica niche, one of which was by Bernini himself.[86] His project is preserved in a workshop drawing in Vienna, which is practically identical with the description given in the craftsmen's invoices (Fig. 48).[87] It establishes the basic solution that was to be retained in the final execution: a monumental statue raised on a high base, in which there are openings giving access to a stairway that leads down to an altar in the grotto below. The statue is conceived in accordance with the traditional formula for St. Veronica, which had appeared on the mediaeval tabernacle (Fig. 8) and would later also provide the point of departure for Francesco Mochi's figure of the saint. Indeed, the whole arrangement, comprising an altar below, depictions of the appropriate saint and relic, and a container for the relic above seems consciously to recreate in relief the reliquary monuments of the old basilica. Since there is no reference in the project to the Lance, which was kept together with the Holy Face, it must already have been determined to house the relics separately.

84. The documents are published by Pollak, 311ff. The inscription bearing the date 1625 placed beneath the balustrade (Forcella, *Iscrizioni*, VI, 148 No. 542) surely refers to the completion of this reconstruction (cf. also Hess, *Künstlerbiographien*, 109 n.1), rather than the beginning of that which followed (Brauer-Wittkower, *Zeichnungen*, 22 n.2).

85. "Vi son' in essere le cimenti p 2 altari da farsi uno sotto al nicchio del Volto S.^{to}, et l'altro di S. And.^{a} Parlarne con N S.^{re} parria molto conveniente far li altari del Volto S.^{to} e S. And.^{a} in d.^{i} luoghi, che non vi son, ne si vuole andare a celebrare ne' luoghi, dove son collocate d.^{e} reliquie." (Minutes of the Congregation, June 3, 1626; transcribed from the original, Arch. Fabb. S. P., I Piano, Ser. 2, Vol. 71, *Congregazioni* 1571–1630, fol. 397r)

    Cf. Baldinucci, *Vita,* 165f. Bernini was accused of having weakened the piers, causing cracks that had appeared in the dome.

86. The documents are quoted in Pollak, 465f., but are there misleadingly placed under the heading of the upper reliquary niches.

87. Apparently overlooking the correspondence with the documents, Brauer and Wittkower regarded the project as the invention of another artist (*Zeichnungen,* 23 n.3, pl. 195a). I quote the documents after Pollak, 24, 29f. (italics mine):

    Per un'altro Modello sotto la Nicchia del Volto Santo con il disegnio del Sr Cav^r Bernino *fatto amezzo ottangolo con pilastri alli angoli* doppij con basamento, zoccolo con li collarino fregi cimasa tutto scorniciato fatto tutte le modinature etc. . . . *con il finimento sopra fatto à piramida con le mozzole* (mensole?) *nelle Cantonate* alto tutto p^i 32 long. di giro p^i 30 etc. . . . Δ 80
    Per li fusti contornati dove è dipinta *la Veronica e doi angeli grandi* etc. . . . Δ 10

    . . . .

    E più ordine del Sig^r Chavaglier Bernino si è depinto un modello fatto di legniame sotto alla nichia del Volto Santo con haverlo incessato e stuchato e dato di piacha (biacca) fina e si è inbrunito da alto e passo e svenato di marmaro con un arme del' Papa di chiaro e scuro e quadro cartelone con le steste di carobini messe di rame battuto e unbrato di sopra et dui ferate messe di rame battuto e unbrato di sopra *e una ficura di Santa Veronicha di palmi quindici con dui Angeli di palmi nove messo* di rame battute e umbrato e scorniciato di dutto . . .
    Δ 50

    E più per haver rifatto sopra li ideso modello se è alzato tre palmi di piu è pisogniato restauralo e far di nuovo et un arme del Papa messo di rame battuto umbrato di sopra e *si è fatto sopra le dui porte dui ferate* messe rame battute e umbrate con dui candelone di più e dui ferate di più fatte di color di rame scorniciato e unbrato et haver rifatto un a(l)tra volta la figura di palme 12 e li Angeli di palmi 7 e si è rimesso di rame battuto la maggior parte e umbrato di nuovo . . . Δ 35

The official decision to include all four piers in the program was taken in June of 1627.[88] There had been an earlier proposal to treat the four niches uniformly.[89] But coming after the high altar had nearly been shifted toward the apse and after the nave had been added, the new arrangement was a reaffirmation of the centrality of the crossing. Interest still focused primarily on the Veronica and Andrew niches, however, and in April, 1628, several models (*plura modula seu formae*) for them were shown to the Congregazione della Fabbrica, the group of cardinals who governed the basilica.[90] Remarkable insights into the whole development of the crossing are provided by the records of the meeting of the Congregation a month later, May 15, 1628, in which the choice among the projects was made. There are two documents in question: one comes from the notes made by the steward (*oeconomus*) of the Congregation during the actual meeting, the other from the official record of the meeting as it was transcribed from these notes.[91] Variations between the two versions are normally trivial, but that is not the case in the present instance. In the notes made at the meeting it is said that the design which most pleased the pope was that for the *St. Andrew* and that authorization was given to award the commission. In the official transcription the oeconomus specifies that the project chosen was Bernini's. Thus it appears that Bernini's winning design was for the *St. Andrew,* and it was this design that evidently provided the basis for the statue executed subsequently by Duquesnoy. The implications of this point will become evident when we consider the close similarities between Duquesnoy's figure and Bernini's own *St. Longinus.* The *St. Andrew* was in fact the test case for the whole program. Work was begun immediately on the niche proper; Duquesnoy received the first payment for his full-scale stucco model in May, 1629, and the final payment the following November.[92]

In February of 1629, following Maderno's death, Bernini had been appointed architect of Saint Peter's.[93] The overall scheme matured in April of the same year, when the pope gave the basilica a portion of the famous relic of the True Cross, composed of fragments which he had removed from Santa Croce in Gerusalemme and Sant'Anastasia.[94] The significance of this step can best be appre-

88. Pollak, No. 1621.

89. A document of uncertain date reads as follows: "Nelle quattro nicchie grandi che sono alli piloni della Cuppola à canto l'Altar maggiore è pensato di fare due Chori, uno per li Cantori, et l'altro per li Principi, che verranno à veder la messa pontificale, se bene alcuni hanno opinione, che vi staranno bene quattro Altari nelli quali si potranno collocare li quattro Corpi di S. Leoni Papi, che sono nella medesima Chiesa." (Pollak, "Ausgewählte Akten," 73) Siebenhüner connects the "chori" mentioned here with those shown in Cigoli's project (Figs. 25, 26; "Umrisse," 312, where the reference should read "Pollak" in place of "Orbaan").

Siebenhüner's assumption ("Umrisse," 245, 257) that four figures of prophets made for Saint Peter's in the 1550's by Guglielmo della Porta were intended for the crossing piers, has been disproved by W. Gramberg ("Guglielmo della Portas verlorene Prophetenstatuen für San Pietro in Vaticano," in *Walter Friedlaender zum 90. Geburtstag,* Berlin, 1965, 80 n.7).

90. April 10, 1628:
Fuerunt exhibita plura modula seu formae capellarum construendarum in locis subtus SS^{mas} Reliquias Vultus S^{ti} et Capitis S. Andreae quae per Ill^{mos} DD. visa, et diligenter expressa, Iniunxerunt mihi ut illa S^{mo} D. N. deferrem, ut facilius possit ex dictis et alia, quae habet, formula, seu modula sibi magis placitus eligere et Sacr. Cong. eo citius mentem S^{mi} desuper executione demandare. (Pollak, No. 1622)

91. May 15, 1628:
Li disegni delli Altarini, N. S^{re} dice che la Cong^{ne} veda qual più li sodisfaccia et quello si faccia; mostra gradir il S. And(re)a. si potria deputar. qualche delli SS^{ri} Ill^{mi} S. Sisto e Vidone. (Pollak, No. 1623)
May 15, 1628:
Exhibui Ego Oeconomus plura delineamenta depicta pro forma seu modulo parvarum Cappellarum de mente S^{mi} construendarum in loculis Nicchi nuncupatis per me de ordine eiusdem Sanct^{mi} huic Sacrae Congregationi praesentanda ut illis per DD. visis ex eis eligerent quale perficiendum erit, ideò per eos bene inspectis approbarunt ex eis unum ab Equite Bernino delineatum, utque facilius, et citius opus absolvatur, rogarunt Ill^{mos} DD. Cardinales S^{ti} Sixti, et Vidonum, ut curam huic incumbant et quatenus illis videatur mentem eiusdem S^{mi} desuper melius exquirant, et exequantur. (Pollak, No. 1624)
On the minutes of the meetings, see F. Ehrle, "Dalle carte e dai disegni di Virgilio Spada," *AttiPontAcc,* Ser. III, *Memorie,* II, 1928, 19.

92. Pollak, Nos. 1625ff.

93. Pollak, No. 4.

94. Cf. Torriggio, *Sacre grotte vaticane,* 217. The new relic was at first kept with the Volto Santo and the Lance (Severano, *Memorie sacre,* I, 164).

20

ciated by considering momentarily a document of three years before, July 15, 1626, also reported by Baldinucci.[95] It records with respect to the altars then being planned that the oeconomus was directed to determine whether there were in Saint Peter's other relics of the apostles that might accompany the head of St. Andrew; the head of St. Luke was one possibility mentioned. The thought clearly was to pair the Passion relics, the Volto Santo and the Lance, against relics of the apostles. The idea of pairing remained, as we shall see, but the procurement of the fragments of the True Cross early in 1629 shows that a general theme had emerged which required another Passion relic for its completion.

In the Congregation meeting of December 10, 1629, within a month after the model of the *St. Andrew* was finished, the other three artists who were to execute models of their statues were named.[96] Bolgi began his model for the *St. Helen* on July 2, 1631, and Bernini probably began his model for the *St. Longinus* at the same time; Mochi began the *Veronica* model on September 24 of that year. He completed his model on November 29, 1631, and it was viewed by the pope on February 8, 1632; the pope saw Bernini's completed model one week later, on February 15, and that of Bolgi on March 5.[97] Considerable time elapsed before execution of the marbles began, in Duquesnoy's case presumably because he had to wait until the other models were completed; in the other cases there was delay in acquiring suitable marbles.[98] Duquesnoy was the first to begin work, in April of 1633, and the *Andrew* was in place by October, 1639 (Fig. 50).[99] Bernini began only in June, 1635, but the *Longinus* was installed by June, 1638 (Fig. 51).[100] Mochi also began in June, 1635, and his *Veronica* was in place by October, 1639 (Fig. 49).[101] Bolgi received his first payment in January, 1635, and the *Helen* was finished by the end of 1639 (Fig. 52).[102]

The decoration of the upper niches (Figs. 53–56), carried out between 1633 and 1641, brought the program to completion.[103] The niches were based on a design by Bernini (cf. Fig. 68), which involved reusing the ancient columns from the presbytery of Old Saint Peter's. At first the columns were to support triangular pediments, but in the final form the pediments are segmental and the whole frontispiece is bowed inward. Marble putti surmount the pediments, upon which stucco clouds flow down from the surface of the conch.[104] Above, also in stucco, putti carry inscriptions, while inside the frontispieces are marble reliefs of angels and putti displaying images of the relics.[105]

95. "Delli altari del Volto S.^{to} e S. And.^{a} che le pareva si dovessero fare nelli luoghi etc. et ch'io m'informassi s'in S. Pietro vi fusse reliquia insigne di apostolo per poterla accompagnare con la testa di S. And.^{a} / parl.^{e} à D. Bonin . . [?] / testa di S. Luca." (Minutes of the Congregation, July 15, 1626, Arch. Fabb. S. P., i Piano, Ser. 2, Vol. 71, *Congr.* 1571–1630, fol. 417r). Cf. Baldinucci, *Vita,* 166.

96. Pollak, No. 117.

97. The dates are given by Torriggio, *Sacre grotte vaticane,* 206, 219, 283. Torriggio says that the model of the *Longinus* was finished on July 5, 1631, but more likely this was the beginning date. All the artists received down payments of 50 scudi on Dec. 19, 1629, after which there was a delay while work on the niches proceeded. On May 5, 1631, the Congregation decreed that the models be executed (Pollak, No. 1646) and regular payments for them began in Sept. (*Longinus*) and Nov. (*Veronica* and *Helen*), 1631. Final payment to Bolgi was made on March 15, 1632, to Bernini on April 5, to Mochi on Aug. 11, of the same year. Bernini received a total of 500 scudi, Mochi 450, Bolgi 350. Cf. Pollak, 442f., 454f., 461f.

98. Pollak, Nos. 1718ff.; see end of n.174 below.

99. Pollak, Nos. 1654, 1667. G. Baglione, *Le nove chiese di Roma,* Rome, 1639, 38f., speaks of the *Helen* and *Longinus* as in their places, but not yet the *Andrew* and *Veronica*. His dedication to Cardinal Francesco Barberini is dated Sept. 1, 1639.

100. Pollak, Nos. 1787, 1791. The pope had inspected it on May 1 (Fraschetti, *Bernini,* 76). See also n.125 below.

101. Pollak, Nos. 1735, 1747.

102. Pollak, Nos. 1820, 1752. The statue is signed and dated 1639. The document of 1649 mentioned by Fraschetti, *Bernini,* 74, refers to other works by Bolgi in Saint Peter's.

103. Pollak, 467ff.

104. On this device, see n.132 below.

105. With one important exception; see p. 36 below.

Here again, dual reference to the old church and to Jerusalem is evident. The idea for images of the relics and columns in the upper story seems to have come from the earlier reliquary tabernacles, one of which—that of the Volto Santo—actually had versions of the famous twisted columns (cf. Fig. 8).[106] The cornices, like those of the baldachin, are concave and may be related to the reconstruction of Solomon's Temple in the vault of the sacrament chapel (cf. Fig. 40); the notion of surrounding the central altar by the Solomonic spiral columns has a precedent among versions of the Temple, in which the columns were distributed around the Holy of Holies.[107]

The bowed frontispieces are of particular interest, however, since hereafter they appear frequently in Bernini's work, in varied forms, and they become one of the stock phrases in the vocabulary of Baroque architecture. The motif has a complex genealogy, but in this instance Bernini's direct model lay not far from Saint Peter's, in the Church of Santo Spirito in Sassia. The side chapels of this church are, like the reliquary niches of Saint Peter's, semicircular in plan with half-domes. In a number of cases the frames of the altarpieces are curved in adherence to the wall surface. This is the case in the second chapel on the right (Fig. 57), decorated at the altar and in the vault with paintings by Livio Agresti (d. ca. 1580), where the altarpiece is framed by a pair of columns that closely imitate the sacrament columns of Saint Peter's.[108] Here, too, are the broken pediment surmounted by figures, the flat strips that continue the entablature and bases on the wall as if to form lateral extensions of the frontispiece, and other details that appear in Bernini's niches. His major changes were toward unifying the design, by making the horizontal entablature continuous between the columns and echoing the columns in the form of bent pilasters at the angle with the back wall. Also significant is the fact that Bernini gave the frontispiece a less pronounced curvature than the niche itself (Fig. 58);[109] this, together with the continuous entablature, makes the frontispiece seem almost to project from the niche as an independent unit, rather than following its surface as in the Santo Spirito altarpiece.

Perhaps most remarkable is that even in the design for these niches Bernini's interest may have been more than simply formal. The Church of Santo Spirito, and especially the Confraternity of the Holy Spirit whose seat it was, had an ancient and intimate association with the relic of the Holy Face, and hence with Saint Peter's. The relic had once been kept in the church, and in the later Middle Ages, after it was transferred, the popes would carry it from Saint Peter's to Santo Spirito and back again in annual procession. From the latter part of the fifteenth century the custom was reversed and the Confraternity went in procession to Saint Peter's where it had the signal honor of being shown the relic.[110]

106. As noted by Kauffmann, "Berninis Tabernakel," 229. In fact, it seems to have been a common type, as witness the tabernacles with spiral columns in the upper level in Santa Maria Maggiore and San Giovanni in Laterano in the series of prints by Maggi discussed in Appendix I No. 8 (the Santa Maria Maggiore print is reproduced by Armellini, *Chiese di Roma*, I, 286; cf. P. De Angelis, *Basilicae S. Mariae Maioris de urbe . . . Descriptio*, Rome, 1621, ills. on pp. 83, 85, 87); also in Santa Maria in Campitelli (G. Ciampini, *Vetera monumenta*, Rome, 1690, fig. 3 on pl. XLIV opp. p. 181).

107. Cf. the interior of the Temple in a miniature of Jean Fouquet's *Antiquités judaïques* (Perls, *Fouquet*, 248); "reconstructions" of the Temple as a centrally planned structure were also common (see now S. Sinding-Larsen, "Some Functional and Iconographical Aspects of the Centralized Church in the Italian Renaissance," *Institutum Romanum Norvegiae, Acta*, II, 1965, 221ff.).

108. Cf. P. De Angelis, *La chiesa di Santo Spirito in Santa Maria in Sassia*, Rome, 1952, 10; E. Lavagnino, *La chiesa di Santo Spirito in Sassia*, Rome, 1962, 110.

109. The plan of the niches is from Baldinucci, *Vita*, pl. 11 opp. p. 176. Baldinucci's point (pp. 162f.) is that Bernini did not weaken the piers by deepening the niches, but, on the contrary, tended to fill them in; he also notes that the space between the old and the new surface served to insulate the wall from humidity.
   Cf. the niche with double curvature that Bernini created during the same period for the Countess Matilda monument (Fig. 75).

110. See Moroni, *Dizionario*, CIII, 95f. The connections between the Volto Santo and Santo Spirito are recorded extensively by Grimaldi, *Opusculum*, fols. 35ff., 41, 47, 67f., 147ff.

IV. Changes During Execution

THE CROWN OF THE BALDACHIN

During the long period of work on the statues and the niches two major changes were made, both of which radically affected the design and disposition of the crossing. The first of these occurred probably in 1631 while the models for the niche figures were being made. The two semicircular arches that Bernini had intended to place over the columns of the baldachin were discarded and were replaced instead by the familiar twelve curving volutes (four sets of three) decorated with palm fronds; and the great figure of the Resurrected Christ was replaced by the more traditional globe and cross (Fig. 59).[111] It seems that these alterations were motivated at least partly by practical considerations. One of Bernini's critics mentioned earlier, who submitted a project of his own, objected that the original arrangement would be inadequate to support the Christ figure and restrain the columns, and there would be danger of a collapse.[112] Filippo Buonanni says explicitly that it was feared the columns might give way (*laxari*).[113] In fact, the change increased the number of supports, and created groups of pointed arches, raising the crown and making the thrust on the columns more nearly vertical. A series of drawings shows Bernini experimenting with a variety of convex, concave, and mixed curves that would achieve this result.[114] A small and a full-size model of the new crown were made during 1631; the work was unveiled on June 29, 1633.[115] The repercussions of the substitution of the cross and globe for the Christ, which served to lighten the load, will be discussed in Chapter V.

111. Cf. Brauer-Wittkower, *Zeichnungen,* 20f. Their dating for the change is based on a series of payments beginning in April, 1631, to Borromini for detailed drawings (Pollak, Nos. 1274ff.). Payments for models of the new superstructure also begin at the same time (Pollak, 369ff.). The original form still appears on the canonization medal of 1629 (Fig. 32), and is referred to in a poem published that year (Brauer-Wittkower, *Zeichnungen,* 20 n.2).

   The Christ is also mentioned in C. Bracci, *Rime . . . per il ciborio, opera di bronzo fatta inalzare in S. Pietro . . . ,* Arezzo, 1633, 56:

   Sovra quel bronzo in più Colonne alzato
   Dal divo Urbano, e successor di Piero,
   Vedesi pur l'istesso
   Christo resuscitato. (Florence, Bibl. Marucelliana, Misc. 253, int. 3)

   In his preface (p. 44) Bracci only notes seeing the bronze columns on a recent visit to Rome ("Non è molto, che trovandomi in Roma ammirando le quattro Colonne di bronzo, che fanno ciborio in S. Pietro"). It was still being planned to cast the Christ in Jan., 1633, presumably for another destination (Pollak, No. 1248).

   Also unexecuted were seated figures of Peter and Paul to be placed before the balustrade in front of the baldachin, for which Giuliano Finelli made models (cf. Brauer-Wittkower, *Zeichnungen,* 20 n.2). A drawing in the Albertina (Arch. Hz., Rom, Kirchen, No. 768, 321 x 215mm) shows the figures seated on pedestals attached to the balustrade, flanking the entrance to the confessio.

112. Anonymous; quoted n.55 above.

113. Buonanni, *Num. templ. vat.,* 130: *Verum cum mentem Pontificis non explerent, & nimis aeris pondere subjectas columnas laxari posse timeretur, aliam formam . . . Bernini excogitavit.*

114. Cf. Brauer-Wittkower, *Zeichnungen,* pls. 6ff. (See Addenda.)

115. Pollak, 369ff.; the finishing touches were not completed until two years later.

23

Apse
(west)

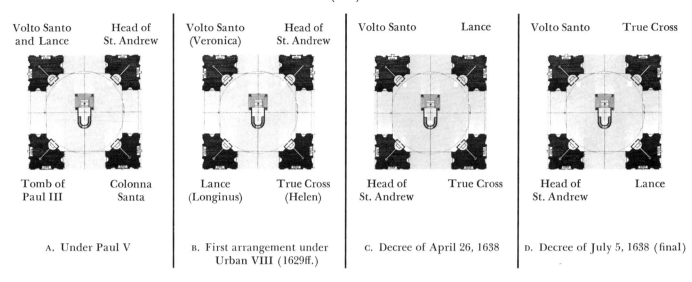

Volto Santo and Lance	Head of St. Andrew		Volto Santo (Veronica)	Head of St. Andrew		Volto Santo	Lance		Volto Santo	True Cross
Tomb of Paul III	Colonna Santa		Lance (Longinus)	True Cross (Helen)		Head of St. Andrew	True Cross		Head of St. Andrew	Lance
A. Under Paul V			B. First arrangement under Urban VIII (1629ff.)			C. Decree of April 26, 1638			D. Decree of July 5, 1638 (final)	

Text Figure. DISPOSITION OF THE RELICS IN THE CROSSING

THE PLACEMENT OF THE NICHE STATUES

The second major change involved the distribution of the relics in the four piers, and hence also the placement of the statues and the decoration of the upper niches. The point of departure for the original placement was certainly the installation of Paul V (Text Fig. A), in which the two Passion relics, the Holy Face and the Lance, had been given the place of honor in the southwest pier (*in cornu evangelii*), while Andrew's head had been placed in the northwest corner, the side of lesser distinction (*in cornu epistolae*).[116] When Urban VIII decided to treat the Lance separately and add the True Cross, the same principle was applied at a lower level to the two eastern piers, that on the south being considered more important than that on the north. Thus, the descending order of precedence of the piers was: southwest; northwest; southeast; and northeast. The Volto Santo, because of its outstanding importance, retained the first place. The distribution of the other three relics depended upon the basic distinction according to which saints are classified, that is, between

116. On the directional symbolism of the Christian basilica, cf. J. Sauer, *Symbolik des Kirchengebäudes*, Freiburg-im-Breisgau, 1924, 87ff.; J. A. Jungmann, *Missarum sollemnia*, Freiburg, 1958, I, 529ff.; I. Lavin, "The Sources of Donatello's Pulpits in San Lorenzo," *AB*, 41, 1959, 20 n.8. The nobler side, to the right of the celebrant of the Mass, gets its name from the fact that the lesson from the Gospel in the Mass was read from there, while the Epistle, of lesser distinction, was read from the celebrant's left. In Saint Peter's the pope celebrates the Mass facing the congregation in the nave. Because Saint Peter's is also "wested" (that is, with the apse in the west), the nobler side is to the south, as it is in normally oriented churches.

117. *Breviarium romanum*, Rome, 1634, *Commune sanctorum*, xviff.

118. The dates are given by Torriggio, *Sacre grotte vaticane*, 200, who also describes the frescoes in detail. An inscription in the vault of the ambulatory between the northeast and northwest chapels reads as follows:

URBANUS VIII • PONTE [sic] • MAX •

NOVOS • ADITVS • APERVIT

ALTARIA • CVM • STATVIS • ER[E]XIT

PICTVRIS • ADAVXIT

ANN • DOM • M • DC • XXXI • PONT • VIII

The inscripion thus dates between Jan. 1 and Sept. 28, 1631 (the eve of the anniversary of the pope's coronation). Payments begin in Jan., 1630 (Pollak, No. 2108), and the last invoice is Jan., 1633 (Pollak, No. 2123).

males and females. In the Common of the Saints, the series of prayers by which saints are collectively venerated, males have preference over females. Apostles and evangelists come before male martyrs; confessors, doctors, and abbots follow, and the female saints come last. Among the latter, saints who were neither virgins nor martyrs—which was the case with Veronica and Helen—constitute the lowest category.[117] By this criterion, Andrew, as apostle and martyr, takes precedence over the male martyr Longinus, who in turn precedes Helen; this was the order in which Urban VIII originally distributed the relics (Text Fig. B). The controlling factor, except for the Volto Santo, was the liturgical rank of the saints, male martyrs *vs.* female non-virgins non-martyrs.

The frescoes illustrating the histories of the relics in the grotto chapels beneath the niches were actually carried out according to this original arrangement, under Bernini's direction, mainly during 1630 and 1631.[118] The liturgical rank of the saints was emphasized in the altar paintings by Andrea Sacchi in these chapels: in the case of Veronica and Helen, scenes showing their connection with the relics were chosen (the Road to Calvary and the Testing of the True Cross), while under Andrew and Longinus the altarpieces pertained to their martyrdom (Andrew worshiping the cross on which he would be crucified and the Beheading of St. Longinus).[119] Another souvenir of the original disposition, in which the liturgical pairing of the saints is also indicated, is in the decorations on the bases of the statues, for which payments were made between April, 1632, and March, 1635.[120] Beneath the inscriptions on the bases in the northwest (Fig. 52) and southeast (Fig. 50) niches are palm fronds, the symbol of martyrdom; they were intended respectively for Sts. Andrew and Longinus. Under Veronica's inscription are laurel leaves (Fig. 49); no change took place here. The base on which Longinus now stands has laurel branches entwining a scepter (Fig. 51), showing that it was intended for the Empress St. Helen.[121]

Most important, it is evident that the statues were conceived as pairs, facing each other diagonally across the baldachin—Andrew *vs.* Longinus, Veronica *vs.* Helen (Figs. 50 *vs.* 51, 49 *vs.* 52). Changing the statues' locations not only destroyed this deliberate opposition but profoundly affected the logic of their design (cf. Text Fig. D). The *St. Andrew,* simply moved diagonally across the crossing, suffered least. But the whole movement in the pose and glance of the *Longinus,* shifted to the opposite side of the nave, is now outward and away from the baldachin; like the *St. Andrew,* it would have been directed inward and up toward the Resurrected Saviour. Likewise, Helen's glance and gesture, now outward in the direction of the transept, would have been inward toward the central axis of the basilica, corresponding to St. Veronica's. The figures thus created a compact, centralized unity that was, in the end, largely dispersed.

---

119. Mosaic copies of the paintings are now on the altars (according to the final, not the original location of the relics). The paintings are now in the Treasury of Saint Peter's. Sacchi received payments in 1633 and 1634 (Pollak, Nos. 2086ff.), and a final payment for the St. Helen scene on Sept. 5, 1650: "Al And.^{ea} Sacchi Pitt.^{e} Scudi 150 m.^{ta} oltre a scudi 650 havuti sono p. intero pagam.^{to} di tutti quattro li quadri che il d.^{o} ha dipinto sotto le grotte compresoci in d.^{o} n.^{o} il quadro con l'hist.^{a} quando Sta helena trovo la Croce di N.S. Sotto à Sta helena di marmo e questo e in conformita di quanto ha ordinato la Sacra Cong.^{e} di q.^{to} di." (Arch. Fabb. S.P., Ser. Arm., Vol. 179, *Spese* 1636–57, p. 276; cf. Ser. 3, Vol. 162, *Decreta et resolutiones* 1642–53, fol. 178r)

    Cf. Fraschetti, *Bernini*, 70; H. Posse, *Andrea Sacchi*, Leipzig, 1925, 54ff.; A. Mezzetti, in *L'ideale classico del seicento in Italia e la pittura di paesaggio* (Exhibition Cat.), Bologna, 1962, 332ff.

120. Pollak, 436ff., 452, 458, 464.

121. A further remnant of the first arrangement is in the motifs that decorate the socle zone of the frontispieces of the reliquary niches; under the twisted columns in three of the niches are Passion symbols (crown of thorns and crossed reeds, gauntlets and lantern, bag of coins, scourges, hammer and tongs, nails and loincloth, ewer and basin), while under those in the northwest niche are various fish, for Andrew the fisherman, whose relic was the only one not connected with the Passion (cf. Figs. 53–56). On the north side of the north column of the northeast niche is an imperial crown with a cross, for the Empress Helen. (I have been able to visit only the eastern niches; hence I cannot identify the emblems on the inner faces of the column bases in the western niches, which are not visible from afar.)

The statues were already nearing completion, and their bases and the frescoes in the grotto chapels had been executed, when, in 1638, the original plan was altered. The motivation was a bull that had been issued by Urban VIII in 1629, when he gave the relic of the True Cross to the basilica. He had then stipulated that the three relics of the Passion be displayed in a sequence that implied an ascending order of importance, the Lance first and the Cross second, climaxing with the Holy Face.[122] A compromise between the original arrangement and the import of Urban VIII's bull was made in the first of two decrees issued by the Congregation concerning the placement of the relics: in April of 1638 the Congregation ordered a new disposition, stating explicitly that it was in accordance with the relative dignity of the relics (Text Fig. c).[123] Yet the decree merely exchanged the places of the head of Andrew and the Lance of Longinus; the preferred position was given to the Lance because it is a Passion relic, but the pairing of the saints was still retained. The difficulty now was that the Lance had precedence over the True Cross. The Congregation changed its mind again and in a subsequent meeting, in July, 1638, decreed what was to be the final arrangement (Text Fig. D).[124] This adheres strictly to the hierarchy of the relics, expressing it in an ascending counterclockwise order beginning with the head of St. Andrew, the only relic not related to the Passion, and ending with the Volto Santo. The pairing of the saints was abandoned completely.[125]

Underlying these changes was a progressive shift in emphasis in which the importance of the relics —rather than that of the saints—became the basis for the arrangement. Hierarchy was the determining factor throughout. In the beginning, however, it was focused on the human "personalities" of the saints represented, which in turn determined their liturgical status; and this is reflected in the design of the statues, which are paired visually and psychologically. Ultimately, the overriding consideration became the relics and their relative dignity; preeminence was given to the mementoes of Christ's sacrifice.

122. . . . *de cetero Ferri primo, deinde Crucis, postremo Sacrae Imaginis reliquiae hujus modi ostendi debeant.* (*Collectionis bullarum*, III, 240 [April 9, 1629])

123. April 26, 1638:
Fuit actum mandato S.D.N., de quo mihi oeconomo fidem fecit Rev.^mus D. Archiep.us Amasiae super collocat.^ne 4.^or p.lium Reliquiarum S.S. Basilicae S. Petri iuxta debitum cuiq pced.^ae ord.em et exhibito Modulo mihi ab eodem R.^mo D. Archie.po consignato et à D. Paulo Alaleona Mag.ro Ceremoniarum eiusd S.D.N. subscripto, in quo p.^s locus Augustissimo Vultus S. Reliquiae in loculo dexterae Parastidis, seu Pilastri subtus Cupolam versa ad Januam facie assignandam proponitur, 2.^s S.^mae Cruci in loculo sinistro sub.to per Diametrum respondente, 3.^s ptiosissimae Lanceae in loculo sinistro p.^o loculo Vultus S.^ti respondente et 4.^s Capiti Gloriosissimi Apostoli S. Andreae in loculo dextero è conspectu S.^mae Crucis. Em.^mi D.ni eodem viso et considerato mandarunt juxta ordinem ibi perscriptum easd S.S.^tas reliquias collocari, et modulum ptum cum p.nti decr.o ad perpetuam memoriam conservari. (Arch. Fabb. S. P., I Piano, Ser. 3, Vol. 161, *Decreta et resolut.*, 1636–42, fol. 36v)

124. July 5, 1638:
Fuit iterum actum de collocatione Reliquiarum pn.lium sacros.^ta Basilicae S.^ti Petri, et non obst.^e Decreto alias facto melius discusso neg.^o resolutum S.^mam Vultus S.^ti Reliquiam in eodem loculo dexterae parastidis seu Pilastri verso ad Januam facie esse collocandam, sacrosanctum Crucis lignum in sinistro eidem respondenti, Praetiosissimam Lanceam in loculo dexterae paristidis, quae invenitur ab ingressu Ecclesiae, et Caput gloriosissimi Apostoli S.^ti Andreae in sinistro huic respondenti. (Ibid., fol. 43v)
The decrees are alluded to by Fraschetti, *Bernini*, 72f.
It is evident that Duquesnoy's cries of foul play at the change of plan, reported by Bellori, Passeri, etc., were quite unfounded (the sources are conveniently quoted in Fransolet, "Le S. André de Duquesnoy," 277ff.; cf. 252).

125. The *Longinus* was installed in June, 1638 (Pollak, No. 1791), before the Congregation's final decree. Presumably the final disposition was known in advance. It is just possible, however, that the statue actually was set up in the northwest pier in accordance with the first decree, and subsequently moved. A list of expenses for work done during June, 1639, includes a payment "per haver condutto il Bassorilievo [sic!] di S. Longino"; this is listed in Pollak as though it were for the statue (No. 1793), though it may refer to the relief of the reliquary niche above (Nos. 1978ff.). The English sculptor Nicholas Stone notes in the diary of his visit to Rome that on Dec. 11, 1639, Bernini told him he would finish within fifteen days a statue on which he was working in Saint Peter's; this can only refer to the *Longinus* (cf. W. L. Spiers, "The Note-Book and Account Book of Nicholas Stone," *Walpole Society*, 7, 1919, 171).

26

The main results and implications of the discussion in the preceding two chapters may now be briefly summarized. First, the statues were planned when the baldachin was to have its original form, with the Resurrected Christ above. Second, it seems clear that besides his own statue Bernini provided initial designs also for the *Andrew* and the *Veronica*. Presently we shall offer evidence that the same is true of Bolgi's *Helen*. Each artist developed the prototype according to his own predilection; but the statues complement one another according to a unified scheme, as we shall also see, and this underlying conception can only have been Bernini's. The significance of these observations will become apparent as we consider the sources and meaning of the figures and the overall program.

In 1637 P. Totti describes the statues (and the long inscriptions below the balconies) as if they were already in place according to the original plan, though none of the figures was completed then (*Ristretto delle grandezze di Roma,* Rome, 1637, 5ff.). The next year he adds a correction, "hoggi si sono mutati i luoghi di S. Longino e di S. Andrea" (*Ritratto di Roma moderna,* Rome, 1638, 530, with dedicatory letter dated Nov. 18, 1638).

Another indication of the date of the change is provided by two payments to the painter Guidobaldo Abbatini. The first was on April 23, 1637, for having painted the inscriptions on the scrolls carried by the angels in the uppermost arches of the reliquary niches (Pollak, No. 2015); the second was on July 29, 1638, for having painted the inscriptions a second time (Pollak, No. 2018).

Because Torriggio states (*Sacre grotte vaticane,* 220, 232, 283) that the inscriptions below the balconies of the Longinus, Andrew, and Helen niches were set up in 1634, the change has been dated too early (Fransolet, "Le S. André de Duquesnoy," 251 n.8; Kauffmann, "Berninis Hl. Longinus," 370). Torriggio makes no mention of any discrepancy between the inscriptions and the chapels below, an anomaly he certainly would not have overlooked or failed to note in his detailed account. Either the inscriptions were not yet really installed, and Torriggio anticipated, or they were first set in place according to the original arrangement and subsequently shifted.

There is an engraved plan of the grottoes (a reworking of an earlier print showing the grottoes in their pre-Urban VIII form; cf. Lietzmann, *Petrus u. Paulus in Rom,* 193, 304, pl. 11), ordered first by Benedetto Drei, "fattore" of the basilica, with inscriptions in the chapels identifying them according to the final disposition of the relics and carrying the date 1635 (e.g. Bibl. Vat., R. G. Arte-Arch. 5.95 unnumbered). But a further inscription says the plan was brought up to date ("ridotta nella forma che al presente si ritrova") by Pietro Paolo Drei, "soprastante" of the basilica, an office to which he was appointed only in Nov., 1638 (cf. Pollak, No. 28).

The *St. Andrew* is shown in the northwest niche in a view of the interior of Saint Peter's in the Prado, signed by Filippo Gagliardi and dated 1640 (A. E. Perez Sanchez, *Pintura italiana del S. XVII en España,* Madrid, 1965, 279, pl. 75). The statue had been installed in Oct., 1639, after the final decree and therefore certainly in the southeast niche. Incongruously, the reliquary niche above the *St. Andrew* shows the relief with the cross of St. Helen.

It should be emphasized, finally, that all this had no bearing on the actual location of the relics; the Passion relics are kept in the Veronica niche and shown from there (see Moroni, *Dizionario,* CIII, 101f.; P. Moretti, *De ritu ostensionis sacrarum reliquiarum,* Rome, 1721, 111), while St. Andrew's head was reserved to the niche above St. Helen. We have a payment for the canopy over the niche of St. Helen in Nov., 1641, that is, long after the final disposition was made, in which it is stated that the St. Andrew relic was kept there (Pollak, 492; cf. 65 No. 54).

V. The Sources and Significance of the Statues

ST. ANDREW AND THE FIRST VERSION OF *ST. LONGINUS*

The decisive change introduced by Bernini into the two-story organization of the piers under Paul V lay in devoting the lower niches to monumental figures of the saints, and the upper niches to representations of the relics themselves. This new arrangement, already implicit in Bernini's *Veronica* project early in 1627 (Fig. 48), involves a much more explicit reference than had obtained under Paul V to one in particular of the reliquary tabernacles in Old Saint Peter's, namely that of Saint Andrew (Fig. 7). A representation of the apostle's head held by angels decorated the upper story, and standing on the altar below was a colossal marble statue of the saint (Fig. 60).[126] The relationship goes beyond general organization, however. The earlier statue, which was added to the fifteenth-century tabernacle in 1570, also seems to be reflected in the figure of the saint executed by Duquesnoy (Fig. 50); the arrangement of the drapery is similar and the figure holds the cross behind him in the same distinctive way. The connection clearly forms part of the pattern of deliberate reminiscences of the old basilica's monuments in the new crossing.

Another antecedent that must be taken into account is an engraving (Fig. 61) from a series depicting the apostles by the Antwerp printmaker Adriaen Collaert (d. 1618).[127] The saint is again placed in front of the cross, which consists of knotty cylindrical logs, and embraces it with his right arm; here, moreover, part of the mantle falls behind the cross at the right side, as in the marble. The link with Collaert's engraving is of special interest because another series of prints by him—a life of St. Theresa printed first at Antwerp in 1613 and then at Rome before 1622—later served as one of Bernini's chief sources for his Chapel of Saint Teresa in Santa Maria della Vittoria in Rome (begun 1647).[128]

The Duquesnoy figure is also inconceivable without still another model, by which the earlier images were brought up to date; this is Domenichino's famous depiction of St. Andrew in Apotheosis on the vault of the choir of Sant'Andrea della Valle (Fig. 62). Domenichino had executed the fresco late in 1624, a few years before Bernini submitted his design for the St. Andrew niche in April,

126. C. De Fabriczy, "La statua di Sant'Andrea all'ingresso della sagrestia in San Pietro," *L'Arte*, 4, 1901, 67ff.

127. The similarity was first noted in print by Hess ("Notes sur Duquesnoy," 30f.), who cites R. Berliner.

128. This relationship will be explored at length in my forthcoming study of the Saint Teresa chapel.

129. The Apotheosis scene seems to have been the first of the frescoes carried out by Domenichino in the choir and pendentives of Sant'Andrea; a payment of 26 scudi in Dec., 1624, evidently refers to it. The main body of the decoration was executed during 1626–27, and the latest payment to Domenichino is in Feb., 1628. See A. Boni, *La chiesa di S. Andrea della Valle* (Conferenza letta all'Associazione Archeologica romana la sera dell'8 Dic. 1907), Rome, 1908, 21; Hess, *Die Künstlerbiographien*, 48 n.5; H. Hibbard, "The Date of Lanfranco's Fresco in the Villa Borghese and Other Chronological Problems," in *Misc. Bibl. Hertz.*, 357f., 364; Borea, *Domenichino*, 184.

130. The pose, gesture, and expression for an upward soaring figure are characteristic of Domenichino and recur frequently in his work (cf. Borea, *Domenichino*, pls. 28, 47, 67, 81f.).

    The statue's connection with Domenichino, though not with the Sant'Andrea fresco, has been noted by J. Pope-Hennessy, *Italian High Renaissance and Baroque Sculpture*, London, 1963, text vol. p. 109, and Nava Cellini, "Duquesnoy e Poussin," 41.

    Nava Cellini (pp. 40f.) revives the attribution to Duquesnoy of a terra-cotta model of St. Andrew in Sant'Andrea delle Fratte, which had been rejected by Fransolet ("Le S. André de Duquesnoy," 243 n.4) and Hess (*Die Künstlerbiographien*, 110 n.1; "Notes sur Duquesnoy," 31f.). The tilt of the head in the opposite direction seems sufficient, in the present context, to exclude it as a study for the Saint Peter's figure; indeed, the model has close analogies to the statue of the saint by Camillo Rusconi in the Lateran (cf. A. Riccoboni, *Roma nell'arte. La scultura nell'evo moderno dal Quattrocento ad oggi*, Rome, 1942, pl. 315).

131. Torriggio, *Sacre grotte vaticane*, 220.

132. The similarity has also been pointed out by M. Fagiolo Dell'Arco, *Domenichino ovvero classicismo del primo Sei-*

28

1628.[129] While the colossal scale and details of pose and drapery come from the earlier sculpture and the engraving, Domenichino provided the basic conception of the saint, with nude torso, head tilted back and to the right, and arms extended upward in a gesture of helpless yearning.[130] As if to acknowledge his debt to Domenichino's work, Bernini had it virtually duplicated soon thereafter on the vault of the chapel under the northwest pier, originally dedicated to St. Andrew (Fig. 63).[131] Indeed, the Domenichino fresco long continued to be an important source of inspiration for Bernini. His vision of the saint rising on a cloud in the apse of Sant'Andrea al Quirinale (begun 1658) seems to translate Domenichino's image into three dimensions (Fig. 64).[132]

The realization that Bernini was responsible for the basic conception of the *St. Andrew*—whose power and monumentality is without precedent or sequel in Duquesnoy's work[133]—helps to clarify its intimate relation to Bernini's own *St. Longinus* (Fig. 51). They are analogous in pose, in psychological expression, and in the arrangement of their drapery.[134] But it must be emphasized that the similarity is not primarily a matter of both works having been conceived by the same artist, nor did it result simply from a desire to set up a harmonious echo between the two statues. Rather, it was created in response to an anomalous situation with which Bernini was confronted when it came to the final execution of his figure.

In its present form the statue represents Longinus as if standing at the foot of the Cross, at the moment when, having pierced Christ's side, he suddenly recognizes Christ's divinity and is converted. He looks up enraptured and thrusts his arms out as if in emphatic imitation of Christ's pose upon the Cross.[135] The fact is, however, that Bernini did not originally plan to represent St. Longinus in this fashion. We have a record of the figure he first intended to pair with *St. Andrew* in one of the scenes in the vault of the chapel in the grotto that was meant for Longinus (Figs. 65, 66).[136] These frescoes, as we have noted, were carried out under Bernini's direction mainly during 1630—beginning in January, almost immediately after the four statues were commissioned—and 1631, with the final payments coming in January, 1633. That the scene dates from early in the campaign is indicated by the fact that the upper niche does not yet show the decoration executed subsequently also on Bernini's design, whereas the design for this decoration, in which the twisted columns support triangular pediments, does appear in one of the frescoes of the Veronica chapel (Figs. 67, 68). This

cento, Rome, 1963, 92.

We may note that it was probably also from Domenichino's frescoes—the allegories in the choir in Sant'Andrea della Valle and the pendentives there and in San Carlo ai Catinari (1627–31)—that Bernini developed his famous technique of stucco spilling over the architectural frame. Bernini is usually credited with the invention of this device, which he introduced in the reliquary niches in Saint Peter's (Figs. 53–56) and elaborated further in his Cappella Pio in Sant'Agostino (begun 1644); in fact, it has a long prior history, with which I hope to deal in my study of the Chapel of Saint Teresa.

The allegory in the choir of Sant'Andrea della Valle variously identified as Hope, Chastity, or Voluntary Poverty seems, along with the figure of Andromeda in the Galleria Farnese, to have contributed to Bernini's figure of Truth in the Borghese Gallery (begun 1646). The painter's influence is evident in Bernini's work as early as the *St. Bibiana* (1624–26) in the Church of Santa Bibiana, which is related to the figure of St. Cecilia in Domenichino's fresco in San Luigi dei Francesi, showing St. Cecilia before the judge (Borea, *Domenichino*, pl. 29).

133. Duquesnoy's only other monumental figure, the *St. Susanna* in Santa Maria di Loreto, is profoundly different in conception (see p. 38 below).

134. Bernini repeated the knot of drapery at the left in the *Countess Matilda* (Fig. 75) and in the Christ of the *Pasce Oves Meas* in Saint Peter's. In light of the documentation concerning the genesis of the *St. Andrew*, the view of the relationship between Bernini and Duquesnoy suggested by Nava Cellini ("Duquesnoy e Poussin," 45, 59 n.47) should be reversed. (See also n.174 below, and Addenda.)

135. Kauffmann has, in my opinion rightly, revived this interpretation of Bernini's figure (cf. his "Berninis Tabernakel," 233; "Berninis Hl. Longinus," 369).

136. The scene anticipates the transferral of the relic to this pier, and is inscribed on the painted frame: *In hoc conditorium Urbano VIII Pont. Max. iussu, solemni pompa Ferrum Lancea infertur;* cf. Torriggio, *Sacre grotte vaticane*, 209.

shows Bernini kneeling before the pope and presenting his drawing for the reliquary niches.[137] Work on the upper niches began in 1633, shortly after the paintings were finished, and it is likely that this sketch dates from toward the end of the campaign in the grotto, that is, the late summer of 1632.

The *Longinus* depicted in the fresco already shows basic elements of the final solution. The figure is oriented toward its right, holding the spear in the extended right hand, head tilted to the side and upward. A huge cloak envelops the shoulders and sweeps forward across the hips. The most notable differences from the final work are the right foot raised on the helmet and the left hand placed across the breast. The figure would thus have been more self-contained and passive than the present *Longinus,* rather more akin in mood, though less so in pose, to the *St. Andrew.* Above all, it is clear that at this stage in the figure's development there was no hint of the Crucifixion simile. In fact, at the time this version was planned to accompany the *St. Andrew,* the baldachin was to be topped not by a cross and globe but by the Resurrected Christ.

These original relationships were evidently based upon a specific tradition in which Andrew and Longinus had long been closely linked. The tradition centered at Mantua, where in the Church of Sant'Andrea is preserved the relic of the Precious Blood of Christ, which Longinus was supposed to have collected from the wound he had made in Christ's side with his lance.[138] Longinus, who according to one tradition was a native of Mantua, and was ultimately martyred there, brought the Precious Blood with him after the revelation of Christ's divinity at the Crucifixion.[139] Andrew was associated with the relic by virtue of the fact that on two separate occasions, in 804 and 1049, when it had been hidden and its whereabouts forgotten, he had appeared miraculously to bring about its rediscovery. The two saints were also linked through the Holy Lance at Saint Peter's which, having been hidden from the Saracens at Antioch, was recovered in 1098 upon another apparition of the apostle.[140]

This Mantuan tradition had given rise to numerous representations in which the two saints were paired.[141] In most of these, and in images showing Longinus paired with other saints (cf. Fig. 70), the figures are depicted in relation to the relic itself. In the chapel of Sant'Andrea that belonged to the Confraternity of the Precious Blood and the Order of the Redeemer, the wooden ancona decorating the altar wall has carved figures of Sts. Andrew and Longinus in the attic zone; flanking the

137. The fresco is inscribed: *Sacellum Beatae Veronicae cum tribus aliis Urbanus VIII extruendum iubet;* cf. Torriggio, *Sacre grotte vaticane,* 200f.

138. Attention was first called to the Mantuan tradition in this context by Kauffmann, "Berninis Tabernakel," 233f., and "Berninis Hl. Longinus," 365; its *quattrocento* manifestations have been studied by M. Horster, " 'Mantuae Sanguis Preciosus,' " *WRJb,* 25, 1963, 151ff.

139. On Longinus legends, cf. *Acta sanctorum,* Antwerp, 1643ff., s.v. "March 15." The most important compilation of the Mantuan traditions is Donesmondi, *Dell'istoria ecclesiastica di Mantova;* the view that Longinus was Mantuan is maintained by G. Magagnati, *La vita di S. Longino martire cavalier mantoano . . . ,* Venice, 1605, preface.

140. J. Bosio, *La trionfante e gloriosa croce,* Rome, 1610, 121; Severano, *Memorie sacre,* I, 161; cf. Kauffmann, "Berninis Tabernakel," 233.

141. Many are mentioned and reproduced in P. Pelati, *La Basilica di S. Andrea,* Mantua, 1952 (cf. pls. 58, 83, 87, 92, 113f.).

142. The ancona is ascribed to G. B. Viani and datable ca. 1600 (cf. E. Mariani and C. Perina, *Mantova. Le arti,* III, Mantua, 1965, 179, 372, 693, and the bibliography cited there).

143. The Church of Saint Barbara in Mantua was the ducal chapel, and a portion of the Precious Blood had been transferred there (Donesmondi, *Istoria ecclesiastica,* II, 354).

144. Magagnati, *La vita di S. Longino;* on Magagnati cf. Ianus Nicius Erythraeus (G. V. Rossi), *Pinacotheca,* Cologne, 1645, 168f., and E. A. Cicogna, *Illustri muranesi richiamati alla memoria . . . ,* Venice, 1858, 17f. The poem describes the moment of Longinus' conversion as follows (p. 7):
    Onde qual suole Aquila altera, il guardo

altar niche below are twisted columns decorated with eucharistic vine scrolls (Fig. 69).[142] Bernini's general concept is foreshadowed by another work in the Mantuan tradition, which pairs Longinus with St. Barbara:[143] the title page of a poetic life of St. Longinus published in 1605 (Fig. 70).[144] The engraving, signed by Wolfgang Kilian, shows the two saints standing before a frontispiece with a pediment whose sides have a scroll-like curve. St. Longinus, who has thrown off his military garb, holds the lance in his right hand and extends his left; St. Barbara's right hand is thrown across her breast. They look up worshipfully toward the reliquary of the Precious Blood, which is held by two putti. The whole arrangement strikingly anticipates that at Saint Peter's, even to the pairs of winged putti who display the papal and apostolic insignia from the horizontal entablatures between the scrolls of the baldachin (Fig. 59). Of particular interest also are certain examples that seem to reflect a great controversy of the 1460's, concerning whether the blood Christ shed at the Crucifixion was reunited to His body at the Resurrection; if it was, relics of the blood could not be venerable.[145] A famous engraving by Mantegna (Fig. 71) shows Andrew and Longinus flanking the Resurrected Christ—exactly the juxtaposition originally planned for the crossing of Saint Peter's, where the saints were to look up toward the figure of Christ on the baldachin between them.[146]

There was good reason to refer to this Mantuan tradition beyond the simple fact that it provided precedence for linking Andrew and Longinus. Pius II had held a solemn disputation on the subject of the Precious Blood in 1462, and though no final decision was made, his sympathy was entirely with those who affirmed its venerability.[147] It was also Pius II who, in the same year, acquired the head of St. Andrew and had built for it the tabernacle at the entrance to Old Saint Peter's. This fact is duly recorded in the inscription above St. Andrew's niche and in the frescoes of his chapel in the grotto.[148] It is also possible that the reference to Mantua was of more than religious and historical significance. With the death of Vincenzo II Gonzaga in December, 1627, and the extinction of the main Gonzaga line, the already vexed question of the succession to the Duchy of Mantua became critical. The papacy was directly threatened, and this was one of Urban VIII's most pressing concerns during the period in which the statues were being planned. He decreed two extraordinary universal jubilees in the interests of peace, in April, 1628, and October, 1629. But his conciliatory efforts were futile and events soon led to a conflict that was one of the major episodes of the Thirty Years War.[149]

Nel Sol di Verità sicuro assisa
E rapito il contempla, e homai comprende
L'uom'morto vivo Dio, già chiaro scorge
Viva la vita haver la Morte estinta,
Onde esclamò con voce alta e sonante
Veramente di Dio questi era il Figlio.

145. Cf. Pastor, III, 286ff.; Donesmondi, *Istoria ecclesiastica*, II, 11ff. On the possible repercussions of this dispute in the Sistine Chapel and Raphael's *Disputa*, cf. respectively Ettlinger, *The Sistine Chapel*, 83f., and F. Hartt, " 'Lignum Vitae in Medio Paradisi.' The Stanza d'Eliodoro and the Sistine Ceiling," *AB*, 32, 1950, 116 n.6.

146. On the engraving see G. Paccagnini, *et al.*, *Andrea Mantegna*, Venice, 1961, 199. Mantegna also depicted the two saints twice at Sant'Andrea in Mantua, in the tondo of the pediment and in the atrium; in the latter case they were shown with the Ascension of Christ above the portal (*ibid.*, and Donesmondi, *Istoria ecclesiastica*, II, 49). After closing the dispute in 1462 Pius II had ordered that the relic be shown each year on Ascension Day (Donesmondi, *Istoria ecclesiastica*, II, 16).

147. Cf. Pastor, III, 286ff.

148. Pastor, III, 258ff. For the inscription, see Forcella, *Iscrizioni*, VI, 148 n.148. The scenes depicting Pius II's reception of the head are described in Torriggio, *Sacre grotte vaticane*, 222ff.

149. See R. Quazza, *Mantova e Monferrato nella politica europea alla vigilia della guerra per la successione (1624–27)*, Mantua, 1922 (Pubblicazioni della R. Accademia virgiliana, Ser. II, Misc. No. 3) and *La guerra per la successione di Mantova e del Monferrato (1628–31)*, 2 vols., Mantua, 1926 (*ibid.*, Misc. Nos. 5–6). On the pope's role, cf. Pastor, XXVIII, 201ff.

But most important, surely, was the fact that the Mantuan tradition made it possible to relate Andrew and Longinus in a meaningful way to the baldachin and altar, and to the other saints in the crossing. It introduced a distinction—the significance of which will emerge presently—between the upper part of the baldachin, where Andrew and Longinus focus their attention, and the altar below.

ST. VERONICA AND ST. HELEN

Despite their obvious stylistic differences it is evident that the two female statues were also conceived as a pair (Figs. 49, 52). This becomes especially clear when it is recalled that the *Helen* was to face the *Veronica* from the opposite pier (cf. Text Fig. B). Their relationship is with the lower part of the baldachin rather than its crown, and by their poses, glances, and gestures, they form a kind of contrapuntal embrace of the crossing. Both figures stride toward the baldachin in the center: Veronica's face is turned to the worshiper approaching from the nave, while her arms extend the Volto Santo toward the area behind the altar; Helen would have displayed the Nails in the direction of the nave, while her glance was focused on the worshiper in front of the altar.[150] The intensely active role of the *Veronica* and the noble calm of the *Helen* present, furthermore, a clearly calculated contrast.

The *Veronica* was, as we have seen, preceded by an early project by Bernini (Fig. 48); but Mochi's highly personal interpretation seems to owe much to the depiction of Veronica by Pontormo in Santa Maria Novella in Florence (Fig. 72). Mochi was born near Florence and received his early training there under the painter Santi di Tito. His strong allegiance to his Florentine artistic heritage has been emphasized since the earliest biography.[151] It is perhaps relevant that Urban VIII was also a native of Florence, where he received his early education. Mochi's reference to Pontormo's figure may have been considered appropriate because the painting decorated the "Chapel of the Popes" in Santa Maria Novella. It had been executed on the occasion of the visit of Leo X, another Florentine, in 1515.[152] That pope had shown considerable interest in the Volto Santo, and issued bulls concerning its display.[153] Indeed, the pose of Pontormo's figure, the drawn curtains behind, and the accompanying inscriptions seem to allude specifically to the rite of displaying the relic.[154] At the same time, important changes were introduced in the context at Saint Peter's. Through the figure's motion and expression the essentially ritualistic character of Pontormo's image is given a dramatic immediacy which suggests that the Passion is actually in progress.

---

150. It will be seen that the actions of the female figures take the spectator into account, as opposed to the males' complete absorption in the miraculous event above. This, too, reflects the relatively more mundane concerns of the non-virgins non-martyrs, as compared with the male martyrs.

   The kind of contrapuntal composition seen in the *Veronica* and the *Helen* has its immediate forerunner in Bernini's work, in the bust of Cardinal Bellarmino in the Gesù (1623–24); here the face turns with a rapt expression to the worshiper approaching the choir, while the hands clasped in prayer are directed toward the office at the altar. The space is thus charged with a dramatic implication that forms the prelude to Bernini's conception of the crossing of Saint Peter's. See the comments in my "Five New Youthful Sculptures by Gianlorenzo Bernini and a Revised Chronology of His Early Works," to appear in *AB*, 50, Sept., 1968.

151. Cf. Passeri, in Hess, *Die Künstlerbiographien*, 130. The *Veronica* has been compared with a figure from an ancient Niobid group (A. Muñoz, "La scultura barocca e l'antico," *L'Arte*, 19, 1916, 133), and with a figure from a painting by Santi di Tito in the Vatican (J. Hess, "Nuovi aspetti dell'arte di Francesco Mochi," *Bd'Arte*, 29, 1935–36, 309).

152. On the Cappella de' Pontefici and its association with no less than four popes, cf. V. Fineschi, *Memorie sopra il cimitero antico della chiesa di S. Maria Novella di Firenze*, Florence, 1787, 36; for recent bibliography, J. Cox Rearick, *The Drawings of Pontormo*, Cambridge, Mass., 1964, I, 106.

153. Cf. *Collectionis bullarum*, II, 374. Awareness in the early seventeenth century of Leo's interest is indicated by the fact that his bulls are quoted by Grimaldi in his treatise on the Volto Santo, along with a notice from Leo's diarist of showings of the relics on Easter and Ascension Days, 1514 (*Opusculum*, fols. 69r and v).

32

The *St. Helen* by Bolgi, who was Bernini's assistant and close follower, is undoubtedly a far more accurate imitation of the master's model. The presence of Bernini's guiding mind can perhaps best be appreciated by considering the source of Bolgi's statue: a painting of St. Helen by Rubens, his first dated work, executed in 1601–1602 while he was in Rome (Fig. 73).[155] The massive proportions of the figure and its drapery, the pose and gesture with extended left arm, the huge cross projecting diagonally out of the picture space have all been transferred to the marble. The most significant difference is that the heavenward gaze of the eyes has been lowered. But a number of other changes have been introduced as well: notably, the outer swathe of drapery is now pulled to one side and joined at the hip, and the left leg, no longer moving forward, is flexed and to the rear of the right leg. Both feet are exposed and wear clog-like sandals. In part, as we shall see presently, these changes may reflect a study of ancient statuary, but the main inspiration seems again to have come from a work by Rubens: the figure of St. Domitilla in the right wing of his altarpiece in Santa Maria in Vallicella, also painted in Rome, in 1608 (Fig. 74).[156] Between the time that Bolgi completed the model of the *St. Helen* and the time he began the final work, Bernini repeated the basic formula almost exactly in his figure of the Countess Matilda on her tomb in Saint Peter's (begun 1633; Fig. 75);[157] the similarities here include the arrangement of the drapery at the breast, the facial type, even the coiffure. In the *Matilda,* however, the positions of the arms have been reversed, and they are now virtually identical with those of Rubens' *St. Domitilla.* As with the *St. Andrew* of Duquesnoy, Bolgi's *St. Helen* is unique for the artist who executed it, but fits integrally into Bernini's own development.[158]

Rubens' painting of St. Helen hung until the eighteenth century in the chapel dedicated to her in the Basilica of Santa Croce in Gerusalemme, whence Urban VIII removed the portion of the True Cross for the fourth crossing pier in Saint Peter's. Santa Croce has the most ancient and hallowed associations with the mother of Constantine.[159] It was founded in the Sessorian palace, which had belonged to her, and she was supposed to have installed the chapel that bears her name in her own chamber. The church possesses—besides three remaining fragments of the True Cross—a nail, thorns from the crown, and the Title of the Cross, which Helen was believed to have brought back from Jerusalem.[160] Part of the appeal Rubens' work held, therefore, probably lay in what might almost be called the "authenticity" of its location. This may also be the explanation for the marked similarities, in figure type, pose, and drapery arrangement, between Bolgi's *St. Helen* and an authentic

154. The inscriptions are transcribed in F. M. Clapp, *Jacopo Carucci da Pontormo, His Life and Work,* New Haven, Conn.-London, 1916, 124.

155. Now in the Hospital at Grasse, France, along with two companion pictures, *The Crowning with Thorns* and *The Raising of the Cross.* Cf. C. Ruelens, *Correspondance de Rubens,* Antwerp, 1887, I, 41ff.; M. Rooses, *L'oeuvre de Pierre-Paul Rubens,* Antwerp, 1889, II, 281f.; most recently, M. De Maeyer, "Rubens in de Altaarstukken in het Hospitaal te Grasse," *Gentse Bijdragen tot de Kunstgeschiedenis,* 14, 1953, 75ff.

156. M. Jaffé, "Peter Paul Rubens and the Oratorian Fathers," *Proporzioni,* 4, 1963, 209ff.; G. Incisa della Rocchetta, "Documenti editi e inediti sui quadri del Rubens nella Chiesa Nuova," *AttiPontAcc,* Ser. III, *Rendiconti,* XXXV, 1962–63, 161ff.

157. The relationship is so close that, as Wittkower has observed, the *Matilda* has even been attributed to Bolgi, though the documents show he was responsible only for secondary details (*Art and Architecture in Italy 1600–1750,* 2nd ed., Harmondsworth, etc., 1965, 201).

158. The *St. Helen* is Bolgi's only piece of monumental religious statuary. Cf. V. Martinelli, "Contributi alla scultura del seicento. V. Andrea Bolgi a Roma e a Napoli," *Commentari,* 10, 1959, 137ff.; A. Nava Cellini, "Ritratti di Andrea Bolgi," *Paragone,* 13, No. 147, 1962, 24ff.

159. R. Krautheimer, *Corpus basilicarum christianarum Romae,* Vatican, I, 1937, 165ff.

160. Rubens includes the Crown of Thorns and Title of the Cross, Bolgi includes the Nails, and the Title appears in the relief of the reliquary niche above. On the relics in Santa Croce see B. Bedini, *Le reliquie sessoriane della Passione del Signore,* Rome, 1956.

classical prototype still existing in Santa Croce, over the same altar that Rubens' painting once decorated (Fig. 76). When the painting was removed toward the middle of the eighteenth century, it was replaced by an ancient statue restored (chiefly the head and arms) to represent St. Helen in a kind of composite imitation of Rubens and Bolgi. There is good reason to identify the figure now on the altar with a statue of the Empress Helen that had been found in a mid-sixteenth century excavation in the garden behind the church.[161]

Still more important as a key to the relevance of Rubens' painting for the program at Saint Peter's are the Solomonic columns of Saint Peter's that appear in the background. They are employed in such a way—under the arches of a larger building, with no sign of a superstructure and with a drape hanging from the architrave—that might easily suggest a kind of tabernacle. Their presence in the picture is explained by a tradition current at the time the crossing of Saint Peter's was being planned, according to which it was precisely the Empress Helen who had obtained them in Jerusalem.[162]

Shown thus with the columns, Helen is represented as if she were actually in Jerusalem. In fact, this topographical identification is explicit in the very name of the basilica, Santa Croce in Gerusalemme. The identification, moreover, was not merely metaphorical. When Helen returned to Rome, according to the legend, her ship was loaded with the earth from under the Cross that Christ had bathed with his blood. This venerable earth she placed in the lower part of her room, and it thus underlies the pavement of the chapel dedicated to her, of which Rubens' painting was the altarpiece. The story is told in a long inscription in majolica tiles lining the passageway that leads to the chapel. It celebrates a miraculous rediscovery of the Title of the Cross in 1492, which was the occasion for a major restoration of the chapel preceding the one for which Rubens' painting was made. The inscription explains not only the "meaning" of the chapel, but also its implication for Saint Peter's:

> This holy chapel is called Jerusalem because St. Helen, mother of Constantine the Great, returning from Jerusalem in the year of our Lord 321, having rediscovered the insignia of the Lord's victory, constructed it in her own chamber; and having brought back in her ship holy earth of Mount Calvary upon which the blood of Christ was poured out for the the price of human redemption, and by the power of which entrance to the Heavenly Jerusalem was opened to mortals, she filled it to the lowest vault. For this reason the chapel itself and the whole basilica and all Rome deserved to be called the second Jerusalem, where the Lord for the strength of its faith wished to be crucified a second time in Peter, and where it is believed that the veneration of one

---

161. On the statue in Santa Croce, presumably an earlier work reused in the second quarter of the fourth century, see my note, "An Ancient Statue of the Empress Helen Reidentified(?)," *AB*, 49, 1967, 58ff.

162. Panciroli, *Tesori nascosti*, 532.

163. SACRA VLTERIOR CAPPELLA · DICTA HIERVSALEM · Q BEATA HELENA MAGNI CONSTANTINI MATER · HIEROSOLYMA REDIENS · ANNO · DOMINI · CCCXXI: DOMINICI TROPHEI INSIGNIIS REPERTIS: IN PROPRIO EAM CVBICVLO EREXERIT: TERRAQ SANCTA MONTIS CALVARIAE NAVI INDE ADVECTA SVPRA QVAM CHRISTI SANGVIS EFFVSVVS FVIT REDEMPTIONIS HVMANAE PRAECIVM: CVIVSQ VIGORE IN CELESTEM HIERVSALEM MORTALIBVS ADITVS PATVIT: AD PRIMVM VSQ INFERIOREM FORNICEM REPLEVERIT · EX QVO SACELLVM IPSVM ET TOTA BASILICA AC VNIVERSA VRBS: SECVNDA HIERVSALEM MERVIT APPELLARI · APVD QAM [SIC] ET DÑS AD ILLIVS ROBVR FIDEI: IN PETRO ITERVM CRVCIFIGI VOLVIT · VBIQ VNIVS DEI VENERATIO AC FIDES INDEFICIENS: ET DOMINI PRAECIBVS ET PETRI FAVORE: AD VLTIMVM VSQ DÑI IVDICANTIS ADVENTVM IN VRBE SVBLIMI ET VALENTE AC INDE VERIORE HIERVSALEM: CREDITVR PERMANSVRA ·
For the rest of the inscription, cf. Forcella, *Iscrizioni*, VIII, 187. See now I. Toesca, "A Majolica Inscription in Santa Croce in Gerusalemme," in *Essays in the History of Art Presented to Rudolf Wittkower*, London, 1967, 102ff.

164. This vertical distinction may also be reflected in the ornaments of the upper reliquary niches in the piers (Figs. 53–56).The panels of the socle zone beneath the twisted columns contain (with certain exceptions; see n.121 above) symbols of the Passion (crown of thorns and crossed reeds, gauntlets and lantern, bag of coins, scourges, hammer and tongs, nails and loincloth, ewer and basin), while above, on the frieze of the entablature, are (besides

34

God and the indeficient faith, by the prayers of the Lord and the favor of Peter, will remain until the last coming of the judging Lord in Rome, the sublime and mighty and therefore the truer Jerusalem.[163]

The process of what might be called "topographical transfusion" of Jerusalem to Rome is here clearly delineated, and it is linked specifically to the "second sacrifice" in the person of St. Peter.

In imitating Rubens' picture, and creating the same juxtaposition of St. Helen and the Solomonic columns, Bernini was continuing the topographical transfusion to Saint Peter's itself. When we recall the passage in Tiberio Alfarano quoted near the beginning of this study (ch. II, p. 15 above), identifying the setting of the tomb and altar at Saint Peter's with that of the Temple, the cycle of associations is closed.

From all these considerations it is evident that for Bernini the crossing of Saint Peter's had a specific topographical meaning. Both in a real and in a figurative sense it was Jerusalem, the place where salvation was achieved and is continually renewed. This ultimately is the meaning of the baldachin and its crown and of the figures in the piers. The women concentrate upon the Passion and sacrifice at the altar, the men upon the resurrection and redemption above, as if at the very time and place that the events occurred.[164]

THE DEVELOPMENT OF THE *LONGINUS*

When it was determined to replace the Resurrected Christ by a cross and globe, traditional symbols of the universal dominion of Christianity, this original plan for the crossing was no longer tenable. Bernini dealt with the new situation, typically, by exploiting it, finding a solution that expressed his underlying point of view even more vividly than before. He interpreted the cross not simply as an emblem of the Church, but as an allusion to a real event. The sacrifice was now represented twice, in effect, at the altar and above the baldachin, and the *Andrew* and *Longinus* were now to be related to the same theme as were the *Veronica* and *Helen*. It happened that the *Andrew* might easily be understood as an analogue of the Crucifixion. Andrew was martyred by crucifixion, and one of the most familiar episodes of his legend was his having fallen to his knees to worship the cross as he was being led to his death.[165] Thus, although the pose was derived from the apotheosis image of Domenichino, no change was required for the figure to carry the new meaning: that is, not enthrallment at the sight of the Resurrection, but imitation of the Crucifixion. In fact, the executed figure is identical with the full-scale model done while the baldachin was still to be crowned by the Risen

Barberini bees) paired dolphins with scallop shells, early emblems of salvation.

Bernini's interpretation of the crossing as a whole is foreshadowed by the sacrament altar of Clement VIII in the Lateran, which we have seen was also an important part of the pre-history of the baldachin (see pp. 16f. above). In niches flanking the altar, on the back and lateral walls of the transept end (partially visible in Fig. 42), are four monumental statues of Old Testament personages who prefigure the sacrament and the priestly sacrifice (Aaron, Melchisadek, Moses, Elijah). All four figures look toward the altar as if to witness the enactment of the sacrament. The figure on the lateral wall at the right strides toward the altar, in a motion anticipating that of Mochi's *Veronica* (Fig. 42A).

Of considerable interest in this context, also, are the medals of Clement VIII struck in commemoration of the sacrament, which show the altar. In one of these (cited n.81 above) the structure is shown normally, with the silver reliquary relief of the Last Supper situated high on the wall above the ciborium. In a second medal, the scene is enlarged to fill the whole space within the altar (Buonanni, *Num. pont.*, II, fig. XII; examples in the Bibl. Vat. and the Bibl. Nat.). The structure of the altar itself thus serves as the "large upper room" (Mark 14:15; Luke 22:12), with the Last Supper actually taking place inside.

165. A survey of St. Andrew iconography will be found in H. Martin, *Saint André*, Paris, 1928; H. Aurenhammer, *Lexikon der christlichen Ikonographie*, Vienna, 1959ff., 132ff.

Christ.[166] The only difficulty presented by St. Andrew was the relic. St. Andrew's head, alone among the relics involved, had no reference to the Passion. This may explain one of the most remarkable of all the anomalies presented by the crossing: in the reliquary niche above Duquesnoy's statue is represented not the head of St. Andrew, but his cross (Fig. 54).[167]

Seen in this light, the motivation for the change in the *Longinus* becomes clear. The original pose, in contrast to Andrew's, could not be interpreted as referring to the Passion, and a radical reworking of the figure was necessary. This process must have taken place within a relatively short period between the execution of the fresco in the grotto chapel, probably in the first half of 1630, and the beginning of the full-scale model in the summer of 1631. Two intermediate stages have been preserved. In a bozzetto in the Fogg Museum, the figure has been brought very close to the *St. Andrew* (Fig. 77; cf. Fig. 50).[168] Both arms are now extended, and the drapery, instead of being joined at the neck, is knotted under the left elbow, resulting in a cascade of folds at the left hip and in the diagonal sweep across the right leg. The drapery at the right side practically duplicates the corresponding portion on the *St. Andrew*. The right foot is lowered and straightened, resting now on the shield rather than the helmet, which has been shifted to lie beside the left foot.

In some respects, however, the bozzetto is farther removed from the *St. Andrew* than the painted version (Fig. 66). The figure is tall, slim, wiry, and lithe. The knotting of the drapery creates taut, energetic lines of force in contrast to the loosely falling folds in the *St. Andrew*. The flat placement of the right foot gives the figure a second solid support, as against Andrew's tilted foot with toes barely touching the ground. The drapery at the figure's right and the strips of the epaulettes suggest a wind-caught movement. Above all, the right arm, which in both the painted study and in the *St. Andrew* is relaxed, is now thrust outward vigorously. In other words, while bringing the figure closer iconographically, as it were, Bernini introduces elements of an active dynamism that contrast with the gentle receptivity of the *St. Andrew*.

A drawing at Bassano, which seems to reflect a sketch or model by Bernini, probably represents an alternative solution at a slightly later stage (Fig. 78).[169] The drapery is thrown open at the front and the agitated, broken folds intensify the idea of a sudden burst of revelation, barely suggested in

166. An engraving after Duquesnoy's model, dated 1629, is reproduced by Fransolet, "Le S. André de Duquesnoy," pl. IV opp. p. 247.

167. Perhaps this is also the explanation for the fact that the altarpiece in the grotto chapel represents Andrew worshiping the cross rather than his actual martyrdom, as in the case of St. Longinus.

168. Height 52.7cm; Acq. No. 1937.51. First published by R. Norton, *Bernini and Other Studies*, New York, 1914, 46 No. 2, pl. XII; acquired by the Fogg Art Museum in 1937. The bozzetto was analyzed by Kauffmann, "Berninis Hl. Longinus," 369ff. The gilding may be original; the full-scale model of the *Longinus* was colored (Pollak, No. 1774), but evidently the models of the other figures were not.

169. The drawing was first published as an original by C. Ragghianti, "Notizie e letture," *Critica d'Arte*, 4, 1939, XVI fig. 5; and later by L. Magagnato, ed., *Catalogo della Mostra di disegni del Museo Civico di Bassano da Carpaccio a Canova*, Venice, 1956, 40 No. 35. The view that it follows a Bernini study is here adopted from Wittkower, *Gian Lorenzo Bernini, The Sculptor of the Roman Baroque*, 2nd ed., London, 1966, 197.

170. It is perhaps significant that whereas the sources for the other figures were in more or less isolated representations of the saints, the closest parallels for *Longinus* are in scenes of the Crucifixion (cf. those by Giulio Romano and Lorenzo Lotto cited by Kauffmann, "Berninis Hl. Longinus," 367). Wittkower has observed a similarity between Longinus' head and that of the Borghese Centaur in the Louvre (*Gian Lorenzo Bernini*, 37).

171. Symptomatic of this "active" interpretation of the crossing are the inscriptions in the books held, along with swords, as the attributes of St. Paul by pairs of putti on the north and south sides of the baldachin (cf. Fig. 59). (Putti on the east and west sides hold the tiara and keys of St. Peter. These groups, in effect, replace the statues of the two apostles—parts of both of whose bodies were supposed to be preserved at Saint Peter's—that were intended to adorn the balustrade of the confessio; see n.111 above.) The books are open and each contains an inscription on four pages, only partially visible from the floor. On an occasion when the baldachin was being dusted one of the workmen transcribed the inscriptions for me as follows (the portions I was able to decipher confirm his readings):

the bozzetto. The shield has been removed, and certain details of the arrangement of the drapery at the figure's right and the long, billowing edges of folds at the left are retained in the final work.

The executed statue (Fig. 51) unites elements from both these antecedents. Bernini returns to the mass of drapery knotted in front of the body as in the terra cotta. But instead of being pulled into thin lines of tension, the drapery is crumpled into violent disarray, recalling but going far beyond the sketch. The right foot is flat on the ground while the martyr's helmet and the hilt of his sword are at his left. Perhaps most important is a new element: the hipshot pose of all the earlier studies is straightened and stiffened, greatly augmenting the effect of electric excitement. It may be said that whereas in the original version the saint would have played a passive role in the Resurrection, he now plays an active role in the Passion. In this way, while creating a near counterpart of the *St. Andrew,* Bernini depicts through Longinus a contrasting religious experience. Though implying participation in Christ's sacrifice rather than mourning over it, the contrast is analogous to that between Veronica and Helen.

In sum, the substitution of the cross and globe for the Resurrected Christ atop the baldachin had no effect on three of the figures, but it led Bernini to interpret St. Longinus in a new way. The figure, though isolated and free-standing, is portrayed in its traditional narrative context.[170] This very fact indicates, however, that Bernini's attitude toward the crossing as a whole remained unchanged: he still conceived of it as if it were the site of a dramatic action, a second Jerusalem in fact, with Christ really present at its center.[171]

North:

FRA	ATI		LECT	ROMA
TRE	EX•E		EPIST	NOS
IVST	DE•P		B • PAVLI	FRA
IFIC	CEM		AD	EXI

South:

FRA	SUM ᵬ		LECTIO	ROMA
EXI	DIGNA		EPLAE	NOS
QU			B • PAVLI	FRA:
NO			APLI A	TRES

(partially visible in Fig. 59)

Though fragmentary and garbled, the inscriptions clearly refer to two passages in Paul's Epistle to the Romans: *Iustificati ergo ex fide pacem habeamus per Dominum nostrum Iesum Christum* (5:1); *Existimo enim quod non sunt condignae passiones huius temporis ad futuram gloriam quae revelabitur in nobis* (8:18).

The appropriateness in this context of selections from the message to the Romans is evident. It is remarkable, however, that the texts are not quoted alone, but are accompanied by the prefatory phrase *Lectio epistolae beati Pauli apostoli ad Romanos. Fratres:,* which occurs in the missal, as if the liturgy were actually in progress. Both passages are quoted in succession in the Roman missal as alternate readings for the Common of the Martyrs (*Missale romanum,* Rome, 1635, *Commune sanctorum,* xvf.). The content of the passages also bears witness to the basic conception of the crossing that we have described, referring on the one hand to justification by faith, on the other to the sufferings (*passiones*) of·this world. This distinction seems to echo that between the theological and temporal realms implicit in the references to the unity of the faith and the unity of the priesthood in the inscriptions on the friezes below the four pendentives: southwest, HINC VNA FIDES; northwest, MVNDO REFVLGIT; northeast, HINC SACERDOTII; southeast, VNITAS EXORITVR. These inscriptions, in turn, are subsumed beneath the inscription carried out under Paul V on the base of the dome, referring to the foundation of the church: TV ES PETRI . . . (Matthew 16:18–19). See Figs. 1, 53, 54, 59. (For documents for the dome inscription see Orbaan, "Abbruch," 34, 35, 42, 45; I am uncertain of the date of the pendentive inscriptions, but presumably they were added after the time of Urban VIII.)

VI. Conclusion

We have spoken repeatedly of a "program" for the crossing of Saint Peter's. It has by now become obvious that this term is at best an approximation for an evolutionary process that took place over a considerable period and that was never fully realized. There is no evidence to suppose that all the details of the crossing were worked out in advance as a general scheme. The first steps in the reorganization of the relics were taken early in 1624, at the time the new baldachin was begun. Thereafter the two major elements of the plan, the baldachin and the decoration of the piers, developed *pari passu,* each undergoing basic changes long after work began. Even before the models were finished early in 1632, the form of the crown of the baldachin was being altered. And by the time the statues themselves were nearing completion later in the decade, ideas had so changed that they were not even installed in the positions for which they were intended.

Nevertheless, the crucial period for the gestation of a plan that encompassed the entire crossing was probably between June of 1627, when it was decided to decorate all four niches, and December of 1629, when, the relic of the True Cross having been acquired, models of the four statues were ordered. It was then, or shortly thereafter, that Bernini must have supplied the participating artists with their instructions.[172] A crucial question, to which no very precise answer can be given, is how detailed these instructions were. Mochi (1580–1654) was much older than Bernini (1598–1680), a fully matured artist with a long series of monumental works to his credit. The *Veronica* is so deeply imbued with his personality that one can imagine his having received no more (but also no less) than a general orientation concerning the pattern of relationships to be portrayed.[173] The case with Duquesnoy (1594–1643) and Bolgi (1605–1656) was different. Both had worked under Bernini on details of the baldachin, but Duquesnoy had theretofore produced only a single life-size work,[174] Bolgi none. One may suppose that Bernini gave them much more explicit advice. The assumption that their figures are more or less accurate reflections of Bernini's ideas is confirmed by the documentary and stylistic evidence presented earlier, and by the fact that, as we have also pointed out, the Saint Peter's statues are in many respects quite untypical of their work as a whole.

Once it is recognized that the basic conception of the figures must have been Bernini's, what becomes striking is their diversity of mood, psychological as well as stylistic. It is tempting to explain these variations on the basis of chronology. Certainly the *St. Andrew* reached its definitive form first, when the model was finished in November, 1629. But with the acquisition of the True Cross in April, 1629 (a month before Duquesnoy began work on his model), all the constituents of the program were known, and it would be naïve to presume that Bernini did not begin thinking of them

---

172. We know that under Clement VIII, Cardinal Baronio supplied the subjects for the altarpieces in Saint Peter's (Baglione, *Vite*, 110f.), but there is no evidence for such an adviser for the work under Urban VIII. The documents indicate that the pope himself played an active part in the planning.

173. Bernini seems to have agreed with those who criticized the movement of Mochi's figure as improper; at least, he made clever use of the criticism in his crushing answer to Mochi, who had joined the chorus blaming Bernini for the cracks that had appeared in the dome: Bernini felt extremely compassionate toward the forced and belabored agitation of the *Veronica*, since the defect was caused by the wind coming from the cracks in the dome, not the inadequacy of the sculptor (L. Pascoli, *Vite de' pittori, scultori, ed architetti moderni,* 1st ed. Rome, 1730–36; facsimile ed. Rome, 1933, II, 416).

174. A Venus and Cupid, now lost (M. Fransolet, "François du Quesnoy sculpteur d'Urbain VIII 1597–1643," *Académie royale de Belgique, Classe des Beaux-arts, Mémoires,* Ser. II, IX, 1942, 99f.).
    The problem of the relative chronology of Duquesnoy's *St. Andrew* and *St. Susanna* (see recently D. Mahon, "Poussiniana. Afterthoughts Arising from the Exhibition," *GBA,* 60, 1962, 66ff.; K. Noehles, "Francesco Duques-

in relation to one another. He must have had a good idea of what he wanted by the time the commissions were awarded at the end of that year. Except for the changes in the *Longinus* necessitated by the substitution of the cross and globe for the Risen Christ, whatever subsequent development took place at the hands of the individual artists must have started from a nucleus provided then.

Thus, while an evolutionary process undoubtedly took place, the essential differences among the statues cannot be explained simply on this basis. Instead, they bear witness to Bernini's capacity to adapt his expressive means to a particular interpretation of the figure. In each case, as we have seen, that interpretation was conditioned partly by a specific tradition or traditions, partly by the role the figure was to play in the overall program of the crossing. The figure of St. Helen is classical in form and shows emotion with noble restraint, not primarily because it was designed at a certain moment, nor because it was executed by Bolgi, but because it represents the empress mother of Constantine contemplating Christ's Passion.

Apart from the appearance of many motives and devices that recur later in Bernini's work, much of the chronological significance of the crossing in his development lies precisely in this expressive range. Psychological drama had been one of Bernini's chief interests from the beginning, but this had generally taken the form of relatively simple and strident contrasts. Here, the contrasts remain, but the variations are richer and subtler. These observations have a corollary in the realm of style, and help to explain a phenomenon such as the appearance, on the one hand, of violently broken drapery in the *Longinus,* and, on the other, of a pronounced "classicism" in the *Helen.* These apparently contradictory innovations are in fact enrichments of Bernini's formal vocabulary, just as the emotions the figures display are enrichments of his expressive range. The crossing of Saint Peter's marks a vast widening, or, better, maturing, of Bernini's vision.

In the last analysis, however, the chronological importance of the crossing may lie less in the diversity of the individual elements than in the common bond by which they are related. In Saint Peter's, for the first time, Bernini treats a volume of real space as the site of a dramatic action, in which the observer is involved physically as well as psychologically. The drama takes place in an environment that is not an extension of the real world, but is coextensive with it. And because the statues act as witnesses, the observer is associated with them and hence, inevitably, becomes a participant in the event. In this way, Bernini charged the space with a conceptual and visual unity so powerful that it overcomes every change in plan and disparity of style.

noy: un busto ignoto e la cronologia delle sue opere," *AAntMod,* No. 25, 1964, 91; Nava Cellini, "Duquesnoy e Poussin," 46ff.) is greatly facilitated by the knowledge that the design of the *St. Andrew* approved by the Congregation in June, 1628, was Bernini's, not Duquesnoy's (see p. 20 above). All the early biographies of Duquesnoy state that he owed the commission for the *St. Andrew* to the success of the *St. Susanna.* However, the first document mentioning him in connection with the latter work is a payment for marble in Dec., 1629 (execution of the figure did not come until 1631–33), whereas he had begun the full-scale model of the *St. Andrew* by May, 1629 (p. 20 above). If the biographers' story is true, the success of the *St. Susanna* must have been based on a model of some sort. But this need not have been made before 1628, as has been maintained, but only before May, 1629.

Duquesnoy claimed, according to Sandrart, that the *St. Andrew* was delayed because marble was deliberately withheld (by Bernini); cf. A. R. Peltzer, ed., *Joachim von Sandrarts Academie der Bau-, Bild- und Mahlerey-Künste von 1675,* Munich, 1925, 233. The documents show that only Bolgi, Mochi, and Bernini himself were affected by delays in the delivery of marbles (Pollak, Nos. 1722f.); Duquesnoy in fact received his marble and began working long before the others (p. 21 above).

Appendix I

CHECKLIST OF PROJECTS FOR
BALDACHINS, CIBORIA, AND CHOIRS IN
THE APSE OF SAINT PETER'S UNDER
PAUL V AND GREGORY XV (1605–1623)

As far as possible the entries pertaining to structures over the tomb are given first (Nos. 1–15), to those in the choir second (Nos. 16–27). Within this division the order is roughly chronological, except that entries related to the same project are listed together. No. 28 includes projects submitted under Urban VIII in competition with Bernini.

1. *Project for a tabernacle in the crossing and a choir screen in the apse,* anonymous drawing. Bibl. Vat., Arch. Cap. S. P., "Album," pl. 4 (Alfarano, *De basil. vat.,* ed. Cerrati, 25n., fig. 3 opp. p. 48; W. Lotz, "Die ovalen Kirchenräume des Cinquecento," *RömJbK,* 7, 1955, 72ff., 73 fig. 47; J. Wasserman, *Ottaviano Mascarino and His Drawings in the Accademia Nazionale di San Luca,* Rome, 1966, 66 No. 234) (Fig. 29)

   Plan for the completion of Saint Peter's with an oval atrium. Shows a screen with an altar flanked by two columns at the entrance to the apse; two groups of four columns, each group supporting a cross groin, flank the altar in the crossing. The total of ten columns suggests that the ancient spiral columns were intended (cf. n.27 above). Cerrati associates the plan with a manuscript project by the architect Fausto Rughesi, a connection that has rightly been rejected by Lotz. Lotz attributes the drawing to Ottaviano Mascarino and dates it before 1606. The attribution to Mascarino is rejected by Wasserman. A date at the beginning of Paul V's reign—that is, 1605/1606—seems probable, since, as far as we know, the idea of a tabernacle over the tomb and a choir screen with altar in the apse did not appear before that time.

2. *Project for a ciborium in the crossing,* ca. 1620, drawing by Borromini. Vienna, Albertina, Arch. Hz., Rom, Kirchen, No. 1443 (Fig. 14)

   The drawing proposes a ciborium with a polygonal cupola supported by straight columns over the tomb, to which a portal below gives entrance. Four allegories of virtues stand on the attic. The absence of lateral wings shows that it was intended for the crossing. The absence of an altar indicates that the high altar was to be located in the apse, where presumably the ancient spiral columns would be used.

   The project seems certainly to date from early in Paul's reign, since the confessio built during the middle years is not taken into account. In that case the sheet would be a copy by Borromini of an earlier project (omitting the portion beneath the pavement), devised perhaps at the time the arrangements for the tomb and high altar were first being debated, that is, 1605–1606. The author of the project was doubtless Carlo Maderno, architect of Saint Peter's and Borromini's early mentor. The

redrawing may have been made at the end of Paul V's reign, when we know the question was reopened. It would thus be contemporary with another drawing by Borromini (Fig. 28; No. 26 below) of a project under Paul V, also presumably Maderno's, for a ciborium in the apse, of which a model was actually built. It is conceivable, however, that the present redrawing was made a few years later when, in competition with Bernini, it seems another idea of Maderno's was revived (see n.55 above).

Barring the unlikely possibility that, in the original scheme, Maderno contemplated having ciboria with cupolas both over the tomb and in the choir, it is reasonable to associate this project with the one reported by Fioravante Martinelli, in which Maderno would have decorated the high altar with spiral columns and a canopy (see pp. 7f. and n.53 above).

Finally, it should be noted that the design closely anticipates Borromini's later projects for the ciborium and confessio in the Lateran (cf. Portoghesi, *Borromini nella cultura europea,* figs. 263ff.).

3. *Model of baldachin over the tomb,* 1606. Cf. pp. 5f. above.

4. *Canonization of Francesca Romana,* 1608, fresco. Bibl. Vat., Galleria di Paolo V (Taja, *Descrizione,* 456; Siebenhüner, "Umrisse," 309 n.224) (Fig. 19)

   From a series carried out under Paul V. Shows the baldachin of Paul V essentially as in No. 7, though without temporary decorations.

5. *Canonization of Carlo Borromeo, 1610,* engraving by Giovanni Maggi. Bibl. Vat., Coll. Stampe (Figs. 2, 24)

   The apparatus for the canonization was designed by Girolamo Rainaldi, and is described in M. A. Grattarola, *Successi maravigliosi della veneratione di S. Carlo,* Milan, 1614, 218ff. (A payment to Rainaldi for designs, probably for the canonization, is recorded in September, 1610; Pollak, "Ausgewählte Akten," 79 No. 40—not December as given in Orbaan, 79). The strands of lilies wound around the staves are mentioned by Grattarola (p. 229), who notes that medallions with images of the saint were placed above both the east and the west faces of the baldachin. The medallions appear only on the east face here and in the anonymous engraving of the event (No. 6); they are not shown in the Vatican fresco (No. 7). Grattarola does not mention the angels flanking the medallions in Maggi's print, and they are not shown in No. 6.

6. *Canonization of Carlo Borromeo, 1610,* anonymous engraving (Fig. 3)

   Differs from No. 5 in that the kneeling angels flanking the medallion atop the baldachin are omitted here. Also, this print shows tasseled canopies above the upper reliquary niches in the western piers, which are omitted by Maggi. This view corrects the misleading impression given by Maggi that the placards with standing figures of the saint were hung in the upper niches; in fact, they were suspended from the crown-shaped chandeliers. Finally, this engraving omits the dome of the ciborium in the choir, which Maggi includes.

7. *Canonization of Carlo Borromeo,* 1610, fresco. Bibl. Vat., Galleria di Paolo V (Taja, *Descrizione,* 460; Siebenhüner, "Umrisse," 309) (Fig. 20)

Shows the baldachin of Paul V with strands of lilies wound around the staves.

8. *Interior of Saint Peter's,* ca. 1610, engraving by Giovanni Maggi

Shows the baldachin of Paul V with the four angels, essentially as in Nos. 5 and 6. The supports are decorated with spiral windings which, although there are no lilies, suggest a connection with the canonization of Carlo Borromeo.

This is one of a series of ten prints by Maggi illustrating major Roman churches. The first state of these engravings is known only from a set of modern post cards of very poor quality, published by a Roman antiquarian bookshop, now defunct. Subsequent printings of the engravings are known, though with some lacunae and various alterations (Rome, Bibl. Vitt. Em., 18.4.G.23, dated 1651; Rome, Bibl. Palazzo Venezia, Roma. XI.132, dated 1681); in these sets the old baldachin and background have been canceled and replaced by Bernini's baldachin in its final form. The Santa Maria Maggiore print has been published (see n.106 above), as has that of San Lorenzo fuori le mura (A. Muñoz, *La basilica di S. Lorenzo fuori le mura,* Rome, 1944, ill. on p. 71). The engravings were discussed by G. Incisa della Rocchetta ("Due quadri di Jacopo Zucchi per Santa Maria Maggiore," *Strenna dei Romanisti,* 10, 1949, 290f. n.2), to whom I am most grateful for lending me his set of the precious post cards.

9. *Medal of Paul V,* 1617. Bibl. Vat., Medagliere (Buonanni, *Num. pont.,* II, 506f.) (Fig. 21)

The obverse of the medal is inscribed with the thirteenth year of Paul's reign (which began on May 29, 1617, the anniversary of his coronation); it was doubtless struck to commemorate the opening of the confessio (Pastor, XXVI, 402; cf. Siebenhüner, "Umrisse," 308). Torriggio, *Sacre grotte vaticane,* 37, records that several of the medals were inserted alongside the commemorative inscription in the confessio, which is dated 1617 (Forcella, *Iscrizioni,* VI, 144 No. 529). The elaborate engraving after the medal usually reproduced (Buonanni, *Num. templ. vat.,* pl. 48), apart from other changes, shifts the viewpoint and places special emphasis on the baldachin.

10. *Longitudinal section of Saint Peter's,* 1618, vignette on the engraved map of Rome by Matthäus Greuter (Fig. 4)

Gives a view of the baldachin of Paul V, and a sketchy plan of a ciborium and screen in the choir. The ciborium is partially cut off at the bottom of the poorly preserved map of 1618 in the Bibl. Vitt. Em., Rome (reproduced in A. P. Frutaz, *Le piante di Roma,* Rome, 1962, II, pl. 286), but appears complete in the 1625 reprint in the British Museum.

The visible north wing of the screen is represented in the plan as though it were a straight, uninterrupted wall. The ciborium has fourteen columns arranged in pairs roughly in a circle, except that four columns form a straight line at the front.

The design shown here cannot be identified with any other ciborium project known to me.

11. *Canonization of Ignatius of Loyola, et al.,* 1622, drawing. Vienna, Albertina, Arch. Hz., Rom, Kirchen, No. 780 (Fig. 22)

Unfinished. Details of the temporary installation are virtually the same as in Nos. 14 and 15, for which it is evidently a preparatory drawing. The main difference from our point of view is that the baldachin still appears to be that of Paul V; the staves are shown straight and unadorned. No angels are depicted at the base.

12. *Canonization of Elizabeth of Portugal,* 1624, anonymous engraving. Bibl. Vat., Arch. Cap. S. P. (Fig. 23)

Inserted in a manuscript diary of Saint Peter's by Francesco Speroni (*Diarium Vaticanum Anni Iubilaei MDCXXV,* 1626, MS D 14, kept in the Chapter Archive in the new sacristy; cf. Pollak, 96, 635). The print is a variant of Fig. 30 (see p. 10 above). The differences are minor, except that the present version shows the baldachin of Paul V, rather than Bernini's early project. This is particularly odd in view of the fact that the baldachin begun under Gregory XV had been built by October, 1624 (No. 13). The anomaly is perhaps to be explained by assuming that the engraving was done, in anticipation of the canonization, before the latter baldachin was actually erected and before Bernini had fixed the design of his project. In fact, the day of the canonization was evidently not yet determined, since in the inscription below, a blank space appears where "22" is added in Fig. 30; the latter also adds various decorative details that are absent here.

13. *New model for a baldachin,* built 1622–1624

Discussed above, pp. 8f. A payment on June 22, 1622, to the woodworker G. B. Soria is quoted by Pollak ("Ausgewählte Akten," 107), who reports the latest payments, the last on October 11, 1624 (Pollak, Nos. 35, 984ff.). The payments in fact form a continuous series beginning June 18, 1622 (Arch. Fabb. S. P., I Piano, Ser. 1, Vol. 236, *Spese* 1621–23, and Vol. 240, *Spese* 1623–24). Hence there can be no question that the same work was involved. The payments are authorized by Carlo Maderno.

The baldachin is described in a document published by Pollak, No. 35. This account carries the date 1621, which has been interpreted as an error for 1624, when the final payment was made (Pollak, 17 n.l). The date probably indicates, however, that it was intended to begin construction in 1621 (cf. Siebenhüner, "Umrisse," 318), though payments do not actually start until June, 1622. The work may well have been put off until after the quintuple canonization in March, 1622. It seems likely, in any event, that the plan to rebuild the model dates from before the end of Paul V's reign (d. January 28, 1621); this was certainly the case with its counterpart, the ciborium in the choir, for which also the final accounting was made only under Urban VIII (No. 27).

This baldachin is described by Buonanni (*Num. templ. vat.,* 127) as follows: *Nihil tamen Paulo regnante effectum est, sed postquam Urbanus VIII. Pontificiae Dignitatus Thiaram accepit anno 1623. umbellam firmis hastis sustentatam decoravit, quas Hieronymus Romanus suo scalpro foliato opere exornavit, & anno 1625. Simeon Obenaccius Florentinus auro circumtexit.*

14. *Canonization of Ignatius of Loyola, et al.*, March 12, 1622, engraving by Matthäus Greuter. Rome, Archive of Santa Maria in Vallicella (Fig. 5)

    P. Tacchi-Venturi, in *Canonizzazione dei santi Ignazio di Loiola*, 62 n.3, first called attention to this poorly preserved print, of which our Fig. 5 is a detail. Practically identical with No. 15, except that this is inscribed *Superiorum permissu Romae 1622 Matthae' Greuter exc. cum Privilegio* in the frame of the cartouche with the inscription below the central panel. Also, the canopies above the reliquary niches appear more clearly here, and the rectangular edges of the figural representations in the niches are indicated. According to the inscription, the decorations for the canonization were designed by Paolo Guidotti. A preparatory drawing is in Vienna (Fig. 22; No. 11).

15. *Canonization of Ignatius of Loyola, et al.*, 1622, anonymous engraving (Fig. 6)

    Reproduced initially, without a source, by C. Clair, *La vie de Saint-Ignace de Loyola*, Paris, 1890, pl. following p. 422; after him by P. Tacchi-Venturi, in *Canonizzazione*, pl. opp. p. 56 (cf. pp. 62ff.), and Mâle, *Concile*, fig. 57 (cf. p. 100).

    I have been unable to find a copy of this print, which is evidently a variant of No. 14.

16. *Project for a choir screen with an altar*, anonymous drawing. Windsor Castle, No. 5590 (Fig. 34)

    Kindly brought to my attention by Howard Hibbard. A transverse section of Saint Peter's through the transept. Shows a screen across the apse in the form of a triumphal arch with three openings. Two allegorical figures recline in a segmental pediment above the central arch, which contains an altar. Four angels holding candelabra stand on an attic above the main entablature; these provide precedence for the standing angels on Bernini's baldachin and on No. 28c. The use of a flat screen without a domical ciborium over the altar parallels the Uffizi project attributed to Maderno (No. 25). Probably dates from the beginning of Paul V's reign.

17. *Project for a baldachin with spiral columns*, by Carlo Maderno

    Described by Fioravante Martinelli; cf. above, pp. 7f. and n.53. Martinelli notes that this project was intended for the high altar. It was probably to be placed in the choir, since spiral columns are included, as in Nos. 18, 19, 20, etc. The baldachin may well have been meant to accompany Maderno's project for a ciborium with straight columns over the tomb where no altar was envisaged (Fig. 14; No. 2); if so, it would date ca. 1605–1606.

18. *Drawings by Ludovico Cigoli for a ciborium in the choir*, 1605–1606. Uffizi, A2635 (680 x 475mm), 2639r and v (Figs. 25, 26)

    Discussion of these drawings (two plans and an elevation) was an important contribution by Siebenhüner, "Umrisse," 310ff.; cf. V. Fasolo, "Un pittore architetto: Il Cigoli," *Quaderni dell'-*

Istituto di Storia dell'Architettura, No. 1, 1953, 7 nn.4, 6.

Cigoli envisaged an octagonal, domed ciborium placed slightly in front of the apse, supported by ten spiral columns, two pairs at the front corners, three at each of the rear corners; a balustraded screen would have extended back in concave arcs to the corners of the apse. Siebenhüner (p. 316) assumed that Cigoli's ciborium was the one of which a model was actually built. But the gratings in the base and the floor around the ciborium show that Cigoli favored shifting the tomb along with the high altar, a proposal that was rejected (see the Avviso quoted n.16 above).

19. *Model of ciborium over the high altar in the choir*, 1606

    Discussed pp. 5ff. above. Enough of the superstructure of the centerpiece appears in Maggi's engraving (Figs. 2, 24) to show that it was polygonal. Probably there were pairs of columns at the corners, and the centerpiece was flanked by wings with others. We know that this ciborium used spiral columns, and in 1635 we are told that there were ten of them (see the quotations n.27 above). The reconstructed model of 1622–1624 (cf. No. 27) had ten spiral and four additional straight columns. Two very similar projects are known (Fig. 27, No. 20; Fig. 79, No. 23; Appendix II) in which all the columns are spiral, some of them evidently imitations of the originals. It is possible that the 1635 reference is to the reconstructed model of 1622–1624 (cf. No. 27), which certainly had ten spiral columns, rather than the original of 1606, which may thus have had more. Nevertheless, for independent reasons neither No. 20 nor No. 23 can be identified with the model of 1606, though they may well reflect it. The centerpiece also seems to be echoed in No. 28c (Fig. 35). (See Addenda and Fig. 28A.)

20. *Project for a ciborium*, anonymous. Vienna, Albertina, Arch. Hz., Rom, Kirchen, No. 767 (Fig. 27)

    The centerpiece recalls that in the model actually built (Fig. 24; No. 19), though the details of the dome are different. The project is also extremely close to that of Ferrabosco (Fig. 79; No. 23; Appendix II), and shows what the latter must have been like before the alterations made under the influence of Bernini's first project. Two figures, evidently Peter and Paul, stand on the attic.

21. *Model for a choir stall in the apse*, 1618

    Adì 20 8bre 1618. Conto delli lavori fatti per servitio della R:a Fabrica di S. Pietro fatti da mè Gio: Battista Soria.

    . . . .

    Per haver fatto il Modello, per il Choro da farsi in S. Pietro, fatto d'Albuccio scorniciato di noce, fatto à trè ordini per li Canonici et Beneficiati, et Chierici et in pezzi da disfar' tutto, con il Baldacchino fatto con grand.ma diligenza

    m^ta—————————————15

    (Arch. Fabb. S. P., I Piano, Ser. 1, Vol. 14, *Materie diverse*, fols. 232r, 233v)

    The woodworker G. B. Soria built a model for a choir stall of three levels, with a baldachin, presumably for the papal throne;

42

the stall was designed to be dismountable, which indicates that it was intended for the main apse. The model is probably to be identified with the project for a choir, also dismountable and with three levels, by Martino Ferrabosco, recorded in his book on Saint Peter's (No. 22). The model is probably further to be identified with one mentioned in an invoice submitted by Soria early in Urban VIII's reign: "Per il primo modello fatto per le sedie del coro che si diceva fare nela Tribuna —————— Δ 20" (Pollak, 18 No. 35; on the date of the document see above, No. 13).

22. *Project for a choir stall in the apse*, by Martino Ferrabosco (Ferrabosco, *Architettura di S. Pietro*, pls. XXVIII, XXIX; cf. Appendix II)

The plan and elevation show three rows of seats, the perspective view only two. The caption explains that the project was intended to permit shifting the sacristy from its place on the north side of Maderno's nave, where it proved unsuitable, to the place intended for the canon's choir on the south. The stalls were to be dismountable; the reason given for this varies slightly between the manuscript version of the caption—". . . acciò potessero [le sedie] servire per le funtioni Pontificie nelli giorni solenni, et ordinariam.te p il Clero . . ." (Bibl. Vat., MS lat. 10742, fol. 384r)—and the printed version—". . . acciochè l'istesso luogo potesse servire ancore per le Funzioni Pontificie nelle Festività più solenne . . ." The project is probably to be identified with a model for a dismountable choir with three rows of seats built in 1618 (No. 21).

Though Ferrabosco's project was never carried out, it is still the practice in Saint Peter's to erect a temporary choir in the apse when necessary (see n.43 above).

23. *Project for a ciborium,* 1618–1620, by Martino Ferrabosco (cf. Figs. 79, 80)

Ferrabosco's project is discussed in Appendix II. A likely assumption is that it was initially prepared to accompany his scheme for a choir in the main apse, which can be dated with good reason to about 1618 (see No. 21). A *terminus ante quem* of 1620 is provided by the intended publication date of Ferrabosco's volume on Saint Peter's. Discounting the alterations made to the design later in imitation of Bernini's project, it is very close to the anonymous study in the Albertina, Vienna (Fig. 27; No. 20), which may be taken as a general guide to Ferrabosco's original intentions. Both projects probably reflect the model of 1606 (Fig. 24; No. 19). The main difference, apart from details of decoration, is Ferrabosco's addition of an attic story on the wings.

24. *Project for choirs in the crossing and apse,* 1620, by Papirio Bartoli (S. Scaccia Scarafoni, "Un progetto di sistemazione della confessione di San Pietro in Vaticano antecedente al Bernini," *Accademie e biblioteche d'Italia*, 1, 1927–28, No. 3, pp. 15ff.; cf. most recently H. Hibbard and I. Jaffe, "Bernini's Barcaccia," *BurlM,* 106, 1964, 164 n.21, and the bibliography cited there) (Fig. 12)

Bartoli's *Discorso*, richly illustrated, is known in various manuscript copies in Rome: Bibl. Vitt. Em., MS Fondi Minori 3808 (to which our citations refer), and Bibl. Vat., MS Barb. lat. 4512, fols. 16–43. Bartoli proposed constructing a pontifical choir in the crossing, immediately behind and including the confessio and high altar, in the form of a navicella, or boat. In the apse he contemplated a *coro de' canonici*. The tabernacle over the high altar was to be a ship's mast with billowing sail, executed in bronze and decorated with reliefs of the Passion "à foggia della Colonna Traiana" (*Discorso,* int. 1, fol. 5r). The seats in the pontifical choir were to be collapsible, to permit a view into the navicella when it was not in use.

The date of the project, 1620, is provided by a passage in which Bartoli estimates that it could be completed in four years, in time for the jubilee of 1625 (*ibid.*, fol. 23r). The illustrations, engraved by Matthäus Greuter, were completed only in 1623, by Bartoli's nephew. In one of these (*ibid.*, fol. 88), the Barberini coat of arms was added to the ship's rudder, doubtless with a view to submitting the project to Urban VIII in competition with Bernini; the case thus closely parallels that of Martino Ferrabosco's project (Appendix II).

25. *Project for choirs in the crossing and apse,* attributed to Carlo Maderno. Florence, Uffizi, Gab. dei disegni, 265A (Fig. 13)

Shows a choir installation with two altars in the apse; a flat screen in front includes ten (spiral?) columns. In the crossing immediately behind the confessio (shown in its final form) is a rectangular, colonnaded enclosure, presumably also a choir. The altar at the tomb inside the enclosure is shown underground, and no tabernacle appears above. The project may be dated after the completion of the confessio in 1617 (n.35 above); the scheme as a whole is closely analogous to that devised by Papirio Bartoli in 1620 (No. 24).

26. *Project for a ciborium,* ca. 1620, drawing by Borromini. Vienna, Albertina, Arch. Hz., Rom, Kirchen, No. 766 (Fig. 28)

Can be identified with the model painted by G. B. Ricci, who submitted his account early in the reign of Urban VIII (No. 27). The drawing shows ten twisted columns and four additional straight columns (omitting the surface decoration on all of them). The inscription on the frieze shows that the project was designed before Paul V's death (January 28, 1621). The exact time of Borromini's arrival in Rome is not certain. Heretofore, his presence in the city has not been attested before March, 1621, when he appears in the documents of Sant'Andrea della Valle (N. Caflisch, *Carlo Maderno*, Munich, 1934, 141 n.102). Howard Hibbard recently found his name listed among the workmen at Saint Peter's toward the end of 1619 (November 23–December 6) well before Paul V's death; Arch. Fabb. S. P., I Piano, Ser. I, Vol. 218, *Stracciafogli* 1616–22, fol. 57v. We may also note that the scarpellino Leone Garua, with whom Baldinucci reports that Borromini lived when he came to Rome, was killed in a fall at Saint Peter's on August 12, 1620: *Die 12 Augusti [1620] M.r Leo Garovius de Bisone longobardus Car-*

pentarius cecidit ex fabrica S.^{ti} Petri dū metiretur et statim obijt sed prius recepit extremā untionē eius corpus fuit sepultus in hac nr̃a eccl.^{a} (Rome, Arch. Vicariato, S. Giov. Fior., *Liber Defunct.* 1600–26, fol. 61v)

Though Borromini's authorship of the drawing is unquestionable, it is not likely, if only because of his extreme youth and subordinate position, that he was responsible for the project. Most probably, the drawing, like No. 2 (Fig. 14), was made for Carlo Maderno who, as architect of Saint Peter's, signed Ricci's invoice for work on the model.

27. *Reconstructed model for a ciborium in the choir,* ca. 1622–1624

Described in an account of work by the painter G. B. Ricci, undated but submitted in the reign of Urban VIII (Pollak, p. 12). The document makes it clear that this model was a reconstruction of the earlier one (No. 19); it included a lantern, an octagonal cupola ("fattà a scaglione con 8 cartellini scorniciato"), four apostles on the cornice, four frontispieces with the papal arms, an inscription with the pope's name in the frieze, four oval windows, figurative decorations in the triangles of the four arches. In addition, Ricci says he made four columns with fluting and floral decorations, and fourteen pedestals. Candelabra stood on the architrave above the columns, and there was a balustrade around the altar. From another source we know the model had ten of the original spiral columns (see n.27 above).

The model is recorded in the drawing by Borromini in Vienna (Fig. 28; No. 26). This bears Paul V's name in the frieze, which shows that it was designed before his death in January, 1621. Execution was delayed, as in the case of the new baldachin model over the tomb (No. 13), and probably for the same reasons. The account containing the description includes other work by Ricci begun much earlier; payments to him for cartoons of the choir stuccos occur as early as May, 1621 (cf. n.71 above).

28. *Projects made in competition with Bernini,* ca. 1624

A. *Anonymous project for a baldachin.* From *Modo di fare il tabernacolo*

See n.55 above.

B. *Project by Teodoro della Porta*

Two months before payments to Bernini begin, Teodoro della Porta, the son of Guglielmo, in a letter to the Congregation dated May 12, 1624, says that he will make a "disegno e modello del Baldachino e suo sostentamento per l'Altar magg(io)re di S. Pietro che haverà la simetria, e decoro che conviene secondo le bone regole dell'arte dell'Architettura senza far ingombro et impedimento alla veduta della celebratione" (Pollak, No. 1052). In a letter dating before January 1, 1624, he complains bitterly against provisional works in Saint Peter's, "et in particolare nell'Altare magg(io)re che è stato fatto e rifatto quattro volte diversam(en)te con molta spesa sempre buttata via per modo di provisione come hora segue medemam(en)te" (Pollak, 71 No. 60).

I tentatively identify a drawing in Vienna (Fig. 35; No. 28c) with Della Porta's project.

C. *Project for a ciborium,* 1623–1624. Vienna, Albertina, Arch. Hz., Rom, Kirchen, x-15 (H. Egger, *Architektonische Handzeichnungen alter Meister,* I, Vienna-Leipzig, 1910, 12 pl. 29, with attribution to M. Ferrabosco) (Fig. 35)

A domed ciborium resting on spiral columns, closely similar to the centerpieces in Nos. 18–20, 23, 26 (Figs. 26–28, 79). The main differences from the other designs are that the lateral wings are absent here, as is also the drum between the attic and the cupola. Angels are shown standing on the attic above the columns.

I suspect that the drawing is a kind of pastiche based on the earlier projects and incorporating certain of Bernini's ideas. The absence of the lateral wings shows that it was intended as a free-standing structure in the crossing, doubtless for the high altar. But only under Urban VIII was Paul V's decision to move the high altar to the apse rescinded. The project must therefore date either from the very beginning of Paul's reign, before the decision was made, or from that of Urban. That the latter is the case is strongly suggested by the design itself. The absence of the drum above the attic creates a considerably lower proportion than in any of the other known projects for ciboria, whereas in the crossing even more height was needed. The most likely assumption is that the spiral columns shown were not to be the originals but imitations of them on a bigger scale; enlargement of the whole structure permitted elimination of the drum to achieve the lower proportion required when the counterbalancing effect of the wings was lost. The design thus deals with the same aesthetic problem, by similar means, as does Bernini's baldachin (see above, p. 12), but in the form of a conventional domed ciborium. A further point is that the angels on the superstructure serve no function whatever (not even to hold candelabra, as in No. 16), as if they were taken over from Bernini's project and deprived of their *raison d'être.*

If the argument presented here is correct the attribution to Ferrabosco falls, since he died before Urban VIII was elected (Beltrami, "Ferabosco," 24). A possible alternative candidate is Teodoro della Porta, who early in 1624 complained of Bernini's project and offered to design a baldachin "according to the good rules of the art of architecture without obstruction or impediment to the view of the service" (see No. 28B). Interestingly enough, the lantern has an onion-shaped crown which suggests the curvature of the final crown of Bernini's baldachin.

D. *Project by Agostino Ciampelli*

Mentioned by Fioravante Martinelli; cf. p. 11 and n.53 above.

E. *Project by Martino Ferrabosco*

Revised version of the original project; cf. No. 23 and Appendix II.

F. *Project by Papirio Bartoli*

Originally planned in 1620; cf. No. 24.

44

Appendix II

MARTINO FERRABOSCO'S ENGRAVED PROJECT FOR THE SAINT PETER'S CIBORIUM

I have omitted from consideration in the body of this paper a project for the Saint Peter's ciborium that has played an important role in discussions of the history of the monument since the late seventeenth century. This is a design (Fig. 79) recorded in a volume of engravings, plans, elevations, and projects for Saint Peter's by Martino Ferrabosco, published in 1684 by Giovanni Battista Costaguti.[175] The title page of the 1684 edition says that the work was first issued in 1620, and although the engraving of the ciborium bears the arms of Urban VIII (elected August 6, 1623) 1620 has been taken as the *terminus ante quem*. Ferrabosco's activity in Rome is documented with certainty from February, 1613.[176] He was buried on August 3, 1623, during the conclave that elected Urban VIII.[177]

Knowledge of designs such as Cigoli's and the model of the ciborium in the apse (Figs. 2, 24, 26) makes it clear that the engraved project is not nearly so original as had been thought. The domed central feature, the projecting colonnaded wings, the spiral columns are all derived from earlier sources. But the engraving also shows certain elements that closely parallel Bernini's first baldachin. The spiral columns in the engraving are specifically of the "sacrament" type; on the underside of the dome, clouds with rays that may emanate from a dove of the Holy Spirit are visible; the lantern of the dome is covered by a pergola-like cupola with open ribs, and this supports a crowning figure of the Risen Christ. The caption to the plate in the 1684 volume says explicitly that the design was Ferrabosco's, that it was shown to Urban VIII before he built the bronze baldachin, and that comparison with the latter shows it influenced Bernini's design.[178] Filippo Buonanni in 1696 reproduces the project, and adds that the pope rejected it because it occupied too much space.[179]

There is no reason to doubt that a design by Ferrabosco existed and that it was shown after his death to Urban VIII. Bernini had other competition as well.[180] But no copy of the 1620 edition of the *Architettura* has ever been found.[181] In fact, there was no 1620 edition, at least not in the form of a published book. This is evident from a draft for the preface and captions to the *Architettura* preserved in a manuscript of materials by and pertaining to one Carlo Ferrante Gianfattori (*alias* Ferrante Carli), whom Paul V had appointed to write a history of the basilica to accompany Ferrabosco's engravings.[182] This draft is in a uniform hand, but it is clear from the phraseology that the preface was written first by Ferrabosco himself, after Paul V's death (January 28, 1621).[183] Appended to the preface is the following statement: "Quest'opera fù lasciata da Martino Ferrabosco imperfetta ridotta a fine a spese di Mons. Costaguti con disegno d'Andrea Carone."[184] In a passage elsewhere Gianfattori says of Ferrabosco: *iamque universum opus per vices et intervalla distractum ad umbilicum fere perduxerat, cum brevi morbo terris eripitur.*[185]

It is therefore certain that no 1620 edition was actually published, and that the work was not altogether complete when Ferrabosco died. Since the engraving of the ciborium bears Urban VIII's arms it may well have belonged to the unfinished portion.[186] The captions in the manuscript draft are similar to,

---

175. Ferrabosco, *Architettura*, pl. XXVII.

176. Information H. Hibbard. Cf. Beltrami, "Ferabosco," 23; U. Donati, *Artisti ticinesi a Roma*, Bellinzona, 1942, 405ff. The plan of a wooden model for a circular confessio projected by Ferrabosco is reproduced in Buonanni, *Num. templ. vat.*, pl. 45; cf. Beltrami, "Ferabosco," 28 fig. 4. Assuming the attribution is correct, Ferrabosco must have been in Rome at least by 1611, when Maderno's confessio was begun (cf. n.35 above).

177. Beltrami, "Ferabosco," 24.

178. *Ibid.*, 27: "Disegno di Ferrabosco. Questo ornamento è stato fatto da Urbano VIII . . . al quale prima di far l'opera fù fatto vedere il presente disegno, in qualche parte imitato, come dall'opera medesima si riconosce."

179. *Fuerat etiam Pontefici oblata alia ornamenti idea, in qua collocabantur columnae vitineae, quibus olim Divi Petri Confessio extrinsecus ornabantur . . . sed cum Templi Aream nimis in longum protensa inutiliter occuparet, ineptam extimavit.* (Buonanni, *Num. templ. vat.*, 130)

180. See the competing projects listed in Appendix I No. 28.

181. Cf. L. Schudt, *Le guide di Roma*, Vienna-Augsburg, 1930, 155; but see n.186 below.

182. Bibl. Vat., MS lat. 10742, fols. 370ff. The preface was published in part (and with some errors in transcription) by H. Egger, "Der Uhrturm Pauls V," *Mededeelingen van het nederlandsch historisch Instituut te Rome*, 9, 1929, 94f. Cf. also the relevant passage in a manuscript biography of Paul V by G. B. Costaguti the elder in the Costaguti archive, published by Pastor, XXVI, 492.

183. "Ho final.te p grã del S.o Dio tiratala à fine, e distribuite le tavole in più parti . . . havendo fatte vedere alc.e delle pñti tavole alla S.M. di Paolo Vo le qli erano in sua vita finite, gli piacquero in modo, che commandò si attendesse al fine, e volse che fossero vestite d'historiá con persona giudicata p lettere, e p guid.o habile à tanto carico, fù Ferrante Carlo." (Bibl. Vat., MS lat. 10742, fol. 370v)

184. *Ibid.* I have been unable to identify Andrea Carone.

185. Beltrami, "Ferabosco," 28 n.6.

186. There is in the Bibliotheca Hertziana in Rome a volume, acquired after Schudt's publication (*Le guide di Roma*, 1930), with a frontispiece identical to that of the 1684 edition but bearing the following inscription: "Alla S.ta di N.S. P P Paulo Quinto. Libro de l'architettura DI SAN PIETRO nel Vaticano FINITO Col disegno di Michel Angelo BONAROTO ET d'Altri Architetti espressa in piu Tavole Da Martino Ferabosco. In Roma L'anno 1620 NEL VATICANO. Con licenza, e

45

but not identical with those in the 1684 edition. The draft of the caption for a tabernacle that would have been included as plate XXIX shows that it was produced during the early stages of work on Bernini's baldachin; this it praises, and lays no claim to an influence on Bernini: "... hoggi dalla S. di N.S.P.P. Urbano 8° si arricchisce di un baldacchino sostentato da 4 colonne di metallo."[187] A probable *terminus ante quem* for the addition of the papal arms is the death of Mons. Costaguti, Sr. (uncle of the Mons. G. B. Costaguti, Jr., who finally published the work in 1684) on September 3, 1625.[188] By this time, as the engraving of Elizabeth of Portugal's canonization in March indicates (Fig. 30; see above, p. 10), Bernini's project was public knowledge.

This is precisely the period when Gianfattori was working on his history of the basilica, which he also left unfinished. It has been shown that his work on the basilica is an outright plagiarism of Jacopo Grimaldi.[189] A few years later it was reported that Gianfattori was the author of attacks against Bernini concerning the dome of Saint Peter's, and had a mortal hatred of the artist.[190]

Suspicion that besides the addition of Urban's arms the engraving may have been altered in imitation of Bernini's project receives strong support from three considerations. A drawing in the Albertina (Fig. 27) shows a project in which the

essential elements are virtually identical with those in the engraving.[191] Yet it differs from the print, apart from the absence of the attic on the wings, in that precisely the major details which the engraving has in common with Bernini's design —the "sacramental" columns, the open ribbed pergola, the Risen Christ, the Holy Spirit in the dome—are missing. Secondly, the columns in the print are of the "sacramental" type, implying that all but two were to be newly made. It seems more reasonable to assume that Ferrabosco's original intention, as Buonanni specifically states,[192] was to reuse the original columns, and that their decoration in the engraving was either added (if the print was unfinished), or changed. Finally, and most significant, the engraving itself shows a crucial reworking: between the central buttresses of the lantern traces of a globe supported on a tapering base are clearly visible (Fig. 80). Thus, the lantern, the pergola, and the Risen Christ were all an afterthought.

I would suggest that the engraving was initially a project by Ferrabosco for a ciborium-screen, perhaps in conjunction with his project for the choir in the main apse,[193] intended to be placed at the entrance to the apse. When Urban was elected and plans for a permanent structure over the tomb altar in the crossing were developing, the engraving was submitted,[194] after having been finished or altered to accommodate the same symbolism as Bernini's baldachin.

Privilegio." The volume contains the same plates as the 1684 edition, including the ciborium project with the arms of Urban VIII! The differences from the 1684 edition are that there are no text or captions, some of the plates are arranged differently, there is an additional plate (elevation of one of the little domes and the attic), and two plates that have coats of arms in the 1684 edition are without them here. The volume also contains at the end various other engravings of the sixteenth and later seventeenth centuries pertaining to Saint Peter's. The binding is stamped with the arms of Cardinal Francesco Nerli (elevated Nov. 29, 1669, d. Nov. 6, 1670; cf. P. Gauchat, *Hierarchia catholica medii et recentiores aevi*, Regensburg, 1913ff., v, 5).

Ferrabosco's engravings, including the frontispiece, are here clearly in their original proof state, ready for publication. The fact that even here the ciborium bears the arms of Urban suggests that the plate in its first, pre-Barberini state was unfinished.

The coats of arms in other plates in the 1684 edition were added later, but before the publication: on pl. IV, the atrium of Old Saint Peter's, the arms of Card. Vincenzo Costaguti (elevated July, 1643, d. Dec., 1660; Gauchat, *Hierarchia catholica*, IV, 26); on pl. V, interior of Old Saint Peter's, the arms of Card. G. B. Pallotta (elevated Nov., 1629,

d. Jan., 1668; *ibid.*, 23).

187. Bibl. Vat., MS lat. 10742, fol. 375v.

188. Moroni, *Dizionario*, XLI, 263; Pastor, XXVI, 482 n.2, adds some further information on the elder Costaguti. The second G. B. Costaguti later became cardinal.

189. See Ch. Heulsen, "Il circo di Nerone al Vaticano," in *Miscellanea Ceriani*, Milan, 1910, 264ff. On Gianfattori cf. also A. Borzelli, *L'Assunta del Lanfranco in S. Andrea della Valle giudicata da Ferrante Carli*, Naples, 1910.

190. Fraschetti, *Bernini*, 71 n.1: "Le scritture che si vedono intorno alla Cupola di San Pietro derivano da Ferrante Carli, ch'è nemico del Cavaliere Bernino et che vorrebbe vederlo esterminato." (Letter of the Mantuan ambassador, Jan. 3, 1637)

191. Appendix I No. 20.

192. Quoted n.179 above.

193. See Appendix I Nos. 21ff.

194. And rejected because the wings were an obstruction in the midst of the crossing (cf. n.179 above).

46

Addenda

1. To n.27 and Appendix I No. 19
In the first volume of his catalogue of the drawings of Borromini, which has now been published (*Francesco Borromini. Die Zeichnungen,* Graz, 1967, 14, col. 1, n.3), H. Thelen refers to a drawing of the ciborium model built in 1606 in the choir of Saint Peter's. The drawing (Fig. 28A) is part of an album dated 1613–1616 and attributed to the French Jesuit architect François Derand (J. Guiffrey and P. Marcel, *Inventaire général des dessins du Musée du Louvre et du Musée de Versailles. École française,* v, Paris, 1910, 15, No. 3598; it should be noted that the attribution to Derand has been challenged by H. von Geymüller, *Die Baukunst der Renaissance in Frankreich,* Stuttgart, I, 1901, 309f., followed by P. Moisy, "L'architecte François Derand, Jésuite lorrain," *Revue d'histoire de l'église de France,* 36, 1950, 150ff.). The drawing shows the elevation and plan of the centerpiece, and bears the inscription, "plan et elevation de la chapelle quon a fait a S^t pierre sur le grand autel ou il j a huit coulonnes torse et a chaque coulonne un tel piedestal."

2. To n.53
Thelen (*Borromini Zeichnungen,* 98f.) and his collaborators determined that the marginal corrections in Fioravante Martinelli's manuscript guidebook were originally written by Borromini himself, whose penciled handwriting, subsequently erased but faintly visible, they were able to decipher beneath the transcript in ink. In transcribing the original comment on the passage concerning the baldachin, Martinelli inadvertently omitted from the last sentence, recording Ciampelli's criticism, a phrase which explicitly confirms the view (pp. 11f. above) that the fusion of the canopy with the cornices of the columns was part of a deliberate effort to create a hybrid form—"gramatically" execrable—comprising both a baldachin and a ciborium. Borromini's original sentence ran as follows (italics mine): ". . . diceua che le baldacchini non si sostiengono con le colone ma con le haste, et che *il baldacchino non ricor(r)a asieme con la cornice dele colone,* et in ogni modo uoleua che lo regessero li angeli."

3. To n.60
On the Successa medal (Fig. 38) see also Krautheimer, *Corpus basilicarum* (cited n.159 above), II, 1, p. 4 n.1. The doubt expressed by Franchi de' Cavalieri concerning the authenticity of the medal may be dismissed. The question had been raised in De Rossi's time, and the main import of his study was that the medal, far from being unusual as a type, belonged to a large class of such votive pendants. The famous ivory casket from Pola, discovered subsequently, on which the reconstruction of the Constantinian ciborium depends in part, confirms the validity of the structure depicted on the medal, if not also its connection with Saint Peter's. (On the Pola casket, see most recently T. Buddensieg, "Le coffret en ivoire de Pola, Saint-Pierre et le Latran," *CahArch,* 10, 1959, 157ff.) The notion that the medal was found only in 1636 is based on a misreading of Ménétrier's letter, and the possibility that it came from the Verano catacomb was offered by De Rossi purely as a hypothesis, suggested by the representation of the martyrdom of St. Lawrence that appears on the reverse.

4. To n.66
According to the calculations of T. C. Bannister, the Constantinian shrine at Saint Peter's itself reproduced "exactly the size and shape given in The First Book of Kings for the 'Holy of Holies' of Solomon's Temple" ("The Constantinian Basilica of Saint Peter at Rome," *JSAH,* 27, 1968, 29).

5. To n.114
In a paper delivered at the annual meeting of the College Art Association of America, January, 1968, Professor Olga Berendsen pointed out an intriguing precedent for the final version of the crown of the baldachin, in a catafalque erected in 1621 in Santi Giovanni e Paolo, Venice, for the obsequies of Cosimo II de' Medici, of which the crown consisted of similarly curved ribs surmounted at the apex by a regal diadem (*Orazione di Giulio Strozzi recitata da lui in Venetia nell'esequie del Sereniss. D. Cosimo II. Quarto G. Duca di Toscana. Fatte dalla Natione Fiorentina il dì 25. di Maggio 1621,* Venice, 1621, ills. opp. pp. 4, 5, 19). Dr. Berendsen plans to enlarge upon the analogy in a separate article.

6. To n.134
Besides Nava Cellini, see Mezzetti, in *L'ideale classico* (cited n.119 above), 363, and J. Hess, *Kunstgeschichtliche Studien zu Renaissance und Barock,* Rome, 1967, 137.

Illustrations

1. Saint Peter's, view of crossing toward west (photo: Anderson)

2. Giovanni Maggi, *Canonization of Carlo Borromeo, 1610*, engraving. Bibl. Vat., Coll. Stampe

DESCRITTIONE DEL MAGNIFICO ET SONTVOSO TEATRO DI S PIETRO DI ROMA,

3. *Canonization of Carlo Borromeo, 1610,* engraving. (From *San Carlo Borromeo nel terzo centenario,* 580 fig. 10)

VISTA INTERIORE
DELLA CHIESA DI S. PIETRO
IN VATICANO.

Questa parte della Chiesa da fondamenti fatta da PP. Paolo V.

4. Matthäus Greuter, *Longitudinal section of Saint Peter's* (detail of 1625 reprint of 1618 map of Rome). London, British Museum

5. Matthäus Greuter, *Canonization of Ignatius of Loyola, et al.,* 1622 (decorations by Paolo Guidotti), engraving (detail). Rome, Archive of Santa Maria in Vallicella (517 x 366mm)

THEATRVM IN ECCLESIA. S. PETRI IN VATICANO.
Sumptuosissimū hoc Theatrū factū ad instāntiā Cuitatis Matriti Architecto Paulo Guidotti
Burghesio Equite Doctore et pictore egregio varijs pulcherrimis inuentionib, et picturis vitæ et
miraculorum S. Isidori ornatū et summo decore erectū ad solennitatē Canonizationis dicti
Sancti, in quo vna eadem die alij quatuor in Sanctor̄ album relati fuere. 12 Martij 1622

6. *Canonization of Ignatius of Loyola, et al.*, 1622, engraving (detail).
(From Mâle, *Concile*, fig. 57)

7. *Tabernacle reliquary of the head of St. Andrew, Old Saint Peter's*, drawing. (From Grimaldi, *Instrumenta autentica*, fol. 49r)

8. *Tabernacle reliquary of the Volto Santo, Old Saint Peter's*, drawing. (From Grimaldi, *Instrumenta autentica*, fol. 92r)

9. *Tabernacle reliquary of the Lance of St. Longinus, Old Saint Peter's,* drawing. (From Grimaldi, *Instrumenta autentica*, fol. 71r)

10. Constantinian presbytery, Old Saint Peter's, reconstruction drawing. (From B. M. Appollonj Ghetti, *et al., Esplorazioni sotto la confessione di San Pietro in Vaticano,* Vatican, 1951, pl. H opp. p. 170)

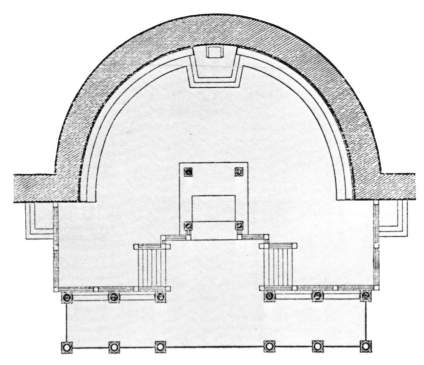

11. Plan of mediaeval presbytery, Old Saint Peter's. (From Appollonj Ghetti, *et al., Esplorazioni,* fig. 136c)

12. Papirio Bartoli, *Project for a choir in the crossing of Saint Peter's* (detail), engraving by M. Greuter. Rome, Bibl. Vitt. Em., MS Fondi Minori 3808, fol. 141 (266 x 197mm)

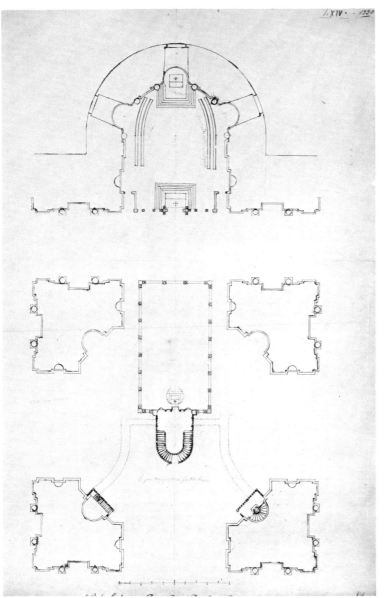

13. Carlo Maderno, *Project for choirs in the crossing and apse of Saint Peter's*, drawing. Florence, Uffizi, Gabinetto dei disegni, A265 (665 x 457mm)

14. Borromini, *Project for ciborium in crossing of Saint Peter's*, drawing. Vienna, Albertina, Arch. Hz., Rom, Kirchen, No. 1443 (254 x 160mm)

15. Medal of Paul II, 1470. Bibl. Vat., Medagliere

16. Ciborium of Sixtus IV (1471–1484), Old Saint Peter's, reconstruction drawing. (From Grimaldi, *Instrumenta autentica*, fol. 160r)

and a bit of unknown design position over altar in the raised of door. kept intact until Clan 1581 [handwritten annotation]

18. Sebastian Werro, *Ciborium of Saint Peter's*, 1581, drawing. Fribourg, Bibl. Cantonale

17. School of Raphael, *Donation of Constantine* (detail showing reconstruction of the Constantinian presbytery based on elements still extant). Vatican, Sala di Costantino (photo: Alinari)

19. *Canonization of Francesca Romana*, 1608, fresco. Bibl. Vat., Galleria di Paola V

20. *Canonization of Carlo Borromeo*, 1610, fresco. Bibl. Vat., Galleria di Paolo V

21. Medal of Paul V, 1617. Bibl. Vat., Medagliere

22. *Canonization of Ignatius of Loyola, et al.,* 1622, drawing. Vienna, Albertina, Arch. Hz., Rom, Kirchen, No. 780 (292 x 195mm)

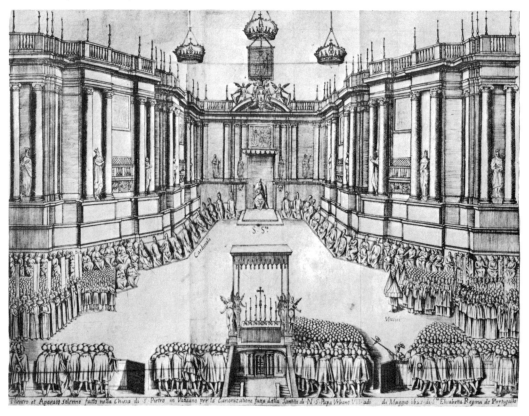

23. *Canonization of Elizabeth of Portugal,* 1624 (decorations by Bernini), engraving. Bibl. Vat., Arch. Cap. S. P. (330 x 245mm)

24. Detail of Fig. 2

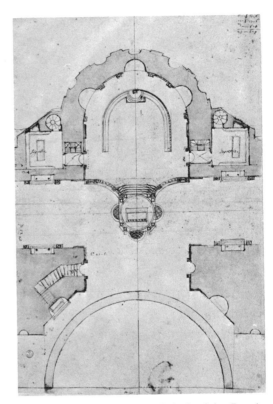

25. Ludovico Cigoli, plan of choir for Saint Peter's, 1605–1606. Florence, Uffizi, Gab. dei disegni, A2639r (424 x 286mm)

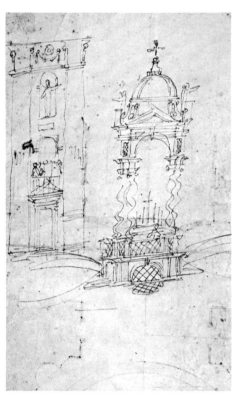

26. Ludovico Cigoli, *Ciborium for choir of Saint Peter's,* 1605–1606, drawing (detail). Florence, Uffizi, Gab. dei disegni, A2639v (424 x 286mm)

27. *Ciborium for choir of Saint Peter's,* drawing. Vienna, Albertina, Arch. Hz., Rom, Kirchen, No. 767 (362 x 315mm)

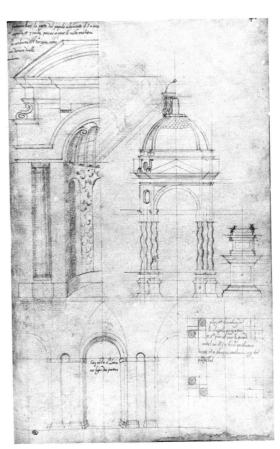

28. Borromini, *Ciborium for choir of Saint Peter's*, ca. 1620, drawing. Vienna, Albertina, Arch. Hz., Rom, Kirchen, No. 766 (235 x 177mm)

28A. Attributed to François Derand, *Ciborium model of 1606 in choir of Saint Peter's*, drawing, 1613–1616. Paris, Louvre, Cabinet des Dessins, École franç. No. 3598 (431 x 300mm)

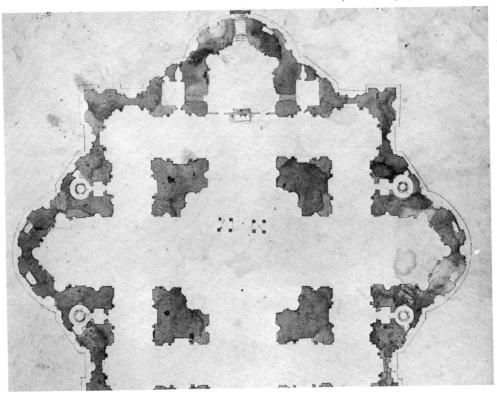

29. *Project for a tabernacle in the crossing and a choir screen in the apse of Saint Peter's*, drawing (detail). Bibl. Vat., Arch. Cap. S. P., "Album," pl. 4 (740 x 455mm)

30. *Canonization of Elizabeth of Portugal*, 1625 (decorations by Bernini), engraving. Bibl. Vat., Coll. Stampe (330 x 245mm)

31. Medal of Urban VIII, 1626. Bibl. Vat., Medagliere

32. Medal commemorating the canonization of Andrea Corsini, 1629. Paris, Bibl. Nat., Cabinet des Médailles

33. *Council of Ephesus,* fresco. Bibl. Vat., Salone Sisto V (1585–1590)

34. *Project for a choir screen with an altar,* drawing. Windsor Castle, No. 5590 (436 x 375mm)

35. *Project for a ciborium,* drawing. Vienna, Albertina, Arch. Hz., Rom, Kirchen, x-15 (525 x 226mm)

36. Giovanni Caccini, ciborium. Florence, Santo Spirito (photo: Alinari)

37. Bernini workshop, *Catafalque for Carlo Barberini*, drawing. Windsor Castle, No. 5613 (485 x 261mm) 1630

38. Early Christian medal. Formerly Bibl. Vat., now lost or disintegrated (from De Rossi, "Le Medaglie . . . ," *Bolletino di Archeologia Cristiana,* 7, 1869, No. 8 on pl. opp. p. 44)

39. Saint Peter's, Chapel of the Holy Sacrament, Altar of Saint Francis

40. Saint Peter's, Chapel of the Holy Sacrament, vault, *Solomon Inspecting the Construction of the Temple*

41. *Altar of the Holy Sacrament, Old Saint Peter's,* drawing. (From Grimaldi, *Instrumenta autentica,* fol. 35r)

42. Rome, San Giovanni in Laterano, Altar of the Holy Sacrament

42A. Rome, San Giovanni in Laterano, Altar of the Holy Sacrament, southwest corner

43. Saint Peter's, view of baldachin and dome

44. Rome, Santa Maria dei Monti, high altar

45. Luca della Robbia, Tabernacle of the Holy Sacrament, 1441–1443. Peretola, Santa Maria (photo: Alinari)

46. Detail of Fig. 42

47. Saint Peter's, mosaics in dome, west side (photo: Alinari)

48. Bernini workshop, *Project for the Saint Veronica niche*. Vienna, Albertina, Arch. **Hz.**, Rom, Kirchen, No. 776 (359 x 305mm)

49. Francesco Mochi, *St. Veronica*. Rome, Saint Peter's (photo: Anderson)

50. Franesco Duquesnoy, *St. Andrew*. Rome, Saint Peter's (photo: Anderson)

51. Bernini, *St. Longinus*. Rome, Saint Peter's (photo: Anderson)

52. Andrea Bolgi, *St. Helen*. Rome, Saint Peter's (photo: Anderson)

SHOWN IN THE ARRANGEMENT ORIGINALLY INTENDED (CF. TEXT FIG. B)

53. Saint Peter's, reliquary niche of St. Veronica

54. Saint Peter's, reliquary niche of St. Andrew

55. Saint Peter's, reliquary niche of St. Longinus
(photo: Anderson)

56. Saint Peter's, reliquary niche of St. Helen

SHOWN IN THE ARRANGEMENT ORIGINALLY INTENDED (CF. TEXT FIG. B)

57. Rome, Santo Spirito in Sassia, Altar of the Virgin

58. Saint Peter's, plan of the reliquary niches. (From Baldinucci, *Vita*, pl. 11 opp. p. 176)

59. Saint Peter's, crown of the baldachin

61. Adriaen Collaert, *St. Andrew*, engraving. Brussels, Bibl. Royale, Cabinet des Estampes

60. *St. Andrew* (from the tabernacle of Old Saint Peter's). Rome, Saint Peter's, Sacristy (photo: Anderson)

62. Domenichino, *Apotheosis of St. Andrew*. Rome, Sant'Andrea della Valle (photo: Anderson)

63. Saint Peter's, vault of northwest grotto chapel (originally dedicated to St. Andrew), *Apotheosis of St. Andrew*

64. Bernini, *Apotheosis of St. Andrew*. Rome, Sant'Andrea al Quirinale

65. Saint Peter's, vault of southeast grotto chapel (originally dedicated to St. Longinus), *Transferral of the Lance of St. Longinus*

66. Detail of Fig. 65

67. Saint Peter's, vault of southwest grotto chapel (dedicated to St. Veronica), *Bernini Presenting the Design for the Reliquary Niches to Pope Urban VIII*

68. Detail of Fig. 67

69. Mantua, Sant'Andrea, Ancona of Chapel of the Precious Blood

70. Wolfgang Kilian, title page of G. Magagnati, *La Vita di S. Longino,* 1605

71. Mantegna, *Sts. Andrew and Longinus with the Resurrected Christ,* engraving. London, Victoria and Albert Museum

72. Pontormo, *St. Veronica.* Florence, Santa Maria Novella, "Chapel of the Popes"

73. Rubens, *St. Helen*. Grasse, Hospital (formerly in Rome, Santa Croce in Gerusalemme)

74. Rubens, *Sts. Nereus, Domitilla, and Achilleus*. Rome, Santa Maria in Vallicella (photo: Alinari)

75. Bernini, monument of Matilda of Tuscany. Rome, Saint Peter's (photo: Alinari)

76. Ancient statue restored as *St. Helen*. Rome, Santa Croce in Gerusalemme, Chapel of Saint Helen

77. Bernini, bozzetto for *St. Longinus*. Cambridge, Mass., Fogg Art Museum

78. *St. Longinus,* drawing after Bernini. Bassano, Museo Civico

79. M. Ferrabosco, *Project for ciborium.* (From *Architettura di S. Pietro*, pl. 27)

80. Detail of Fig. 79

Bibliography of frequently cited sources

Alfarano, T., *De basilicae vaticanae antiquissima et nova structura* (*Studi e testi*, XXVI), ed. M. Cerrati, Rome, 1914.

Armellini, M., *Le chiese di Roma dal secolo IV al XIX*, 2 vols., Rome, 1942.

Baglione, G., *Le vite de' pittori, scultori et architetti* (1st ed. Rome, 1642), facsimile ed., ed. V. Mariani, Rome, 1935.

Baldinucci, F., *Vita del Cavaliere Gio. Lorenzo Bernino* (1st ed. Florence, 1682), ed. S. Ludovici, Milan, 1948.

Bartoli, P., *Discorso sopra una forma di coro per le funtioni ponteficie che si potria fare nel tempio di S. Pietro in Vaticano che riuscira molto vago, et misterioso e pieno di devotione*, Rome, Bibl. Vitt. Em., MS Fondi Minori 3808, interni 1 and 2.

Beltrami, G., "Martino Ferabosco Architetto," *L'Arte*, 29, 1926, 23–37.

Borea, F., *Domenichino*, Florence, 1965.

Brauer, H., and Wittkower, R., *Die Zeichnungen des Gianlorenzo Bernini*, 2 vols., Berlin, 1931.

Braun, J., *Der christliche Altar*, 2 vols., Munich, 1924.

Buonanni, F., *Numismata pontificum romanorum quae a tempore Martini V usque ad annum MDCXCIX*, 2 vols., Rome, 1699.

————, *Numismata summorum pontificum templi vaticani fabricam indicantia*, Rome, 1696.

La canonizzazione dei santi Ignazio di Loiola Fondatore della Compagnia di Gesù e Francesco Saverio Apostolo dell'Oriente. Ricordo del terzo centenario XII Marzo MCMXII. A cura del Comitato romano ispano per il centenarie onoranze, Rome, 1922.

Collectionis bullarum, brevium, aliorumque diplomatum sacrosanctae basilicae Vaticanae . . ., 3 vols., Rome, 1747–1752.

Donesmondi, I., *Dell'istoria ecclesiastica di Mantova*, 2 vols., Mantua, 1612–1616.

Ettlinger, L. D., *The Sistine Chapel Before Michelangelo*, Oxford, 1965.

Ferrabosco, M., *Architettura della basilica di S. Pietro . . . posta in luce l'anno MDCXX. Di nuovo dato alle stampe da Mons. Gio. Battista Costaguti . . .*, Rome, 1684.

Forcella, V., *Iscrizioni delle chiese e d'altri edificii di Roma*, 14 vols., Rome, 1869–1884.

Fransolet, M., "Le S. André de François Duquesnoy, à la Basilique de S. Pierre au Vatican 1629–1640," *B de l'Institut historique belge de Rome*, 13, 1933, 227–286.

Fraschetti, S., *Il Bernini*, Milan, 1900.

Grimaldi, J., *Instrumenta autentica translationum sanctorum corporum & sacrarum reliquiarum . . . 1619*, 2 vols., Rome, Bibl. Vat., MS Barb. lat. 2733.

————, *Opusculum de sacrosancto Veronicae sudario, de lancea . . .*, 1618, Rome, Bibl. Vat., Archivio del Capitolo di S. Pietro, MS H 3.

Hess, J., "Notes sur le sculpteur François Duquesnoy," *La revue de l'art*, 69, 1936, 21–36.

————, ed., *Die Künstlerbiographien von Giovanni Battista Passeri*, Leipzig-Vienna, 1934.

Kauffmann, H., "Berninis Hl. Longinus," in *Miscellaneae Bibliothecae Hertzianae*, Munich, 1961, 366–374.

————, "Berninis Tabernakel," *MünchJb*, 6, 1955, 222–242.

Magnuson, T., *Studies in Roman Quattrocento Architecture* (*Figura*, IX), Stockholm, 1958.

Il modo di fare il tabernacolo, ò vero baldachino, Rome, Bibl. Vat., MS Barb. lat. 4344, fols. 26r and v.

Moroni, G., *Dizionario di erudizione storico-ecclesiastica da S. Pietro sino ai nostri giorni*, 103 vols., Rome, 1840–1861.

Nava Cellini, A., "Duquesnoy e Poussin: Nuovi contributi," *Paragone*, 17, No. 195, 1966, 30–59.

Orbaan, J. A. F., "Der Abbruch Alt-Sankt Peters 1605–1615," *JPKS*, 39, 1919, Beiheft.

————, *Documenti sul barocco in Roma*, Rome, 1920.

Panciroli, O., *Tesori nascosti dell'alma città di Roma*, Rome, 1625.

Pastor, L., *The History of the Popes*, 40 vols., London, 1923–1953.

Pollak, O., "Ausgewählte Akten zur Geschichte der römischen Peterskirche (1535–1621)," *JPKS*, 36, 1915, Beiheft.

————, *Die Kunsttätigkeit unter Urban VIII*, ed. D. Frey *et al.*, 2 vols., Vienna, 1928–1931.

San Carlo Borromeo nel terzo centenario della canonizzazione MDCX–MCMX (Periodical published November, 1908–December, 1910).

Severano, G., *Memorie sacre delle sette chiese di Roma*, 2 vols., Rome, 1630.

Siebenhüner, H., "Umrisse zur Geschichte der Ausstattung von St. Peter in Rom von Paul III bis Paul V (1547–1606)," in *Festschrift für Hans Sedlmayr*, Munich, 1962, 229–320.

Taja, A., *Descrizione del palazzo apostolico vaticano*, Rome, 1750.

Torriggio, F. M., *Le sacre grotte vaticane*, Rome, 1635.